THE
BOOK OF
CATHOLIC
WISDOM

2000 YEARS OF
SPIRITUAL WRITING

THE
BOOK OF
CATHOLIC
WISDOM

Compiled by
TERESA DE BERTODANO

Foreword by
CARDINAL BASIL HUME

LOYOLAPRESS.
CHICAGO

LOYOLAPRESS.

3441 N. ASHLAND AVENUE
CHICAGO, ILLINOIS 60657

Published in 2001 by Loyola Press
This collection © 1999 Teresa de Bertodano
All rights reserved

First published in 1999 by Darton, Longman and Todd, Ltd.,
London, U.K.

Interior design by Rose Design, Carol Sawyer
Interior art by Laura Montenegro

Library of Congress Cataloging-in-Publication Data

The book of Catholic wisdom : two thousand years of spiritual
writing / compiled by Teresa de Bertodano ; foreword by
Basil Hume.
p. cm.
Includes index.
ISBN 0-8294-1488-6
1. Spiritual life—Catholic Church—Quotations, maxims, etc.
I. De Bertodano, Teresa.

BX2350.3 .B66 2001
282—dc21   00-059882

Printed in the United States of America

00 01 02 03 04 / 10 9 8 7 6 5 4 3 2 1

*For those who have
carried this anthology in their
prayers and in thanksgiving
to Mater Admirabilis*

CONTENTS

FOREWORD

What is it that makes life worth living? For most of us, the answer is likely to be "loving relationships"—caring for others and being cared for by them. Here lies the path to human wholeness, and wholeness is very much a part of holiness.

The men and women we meet in *The Book of Catholic Wisdom* are both whole and holy—life givers and life enhancers. If we were to ask any of them the meaning of life, I think they might tell us that life is about being fully alive, both here and in the hereafter. Some of those we meet here are widely known—Augustine of Hippo, Julian of Norwich, Teresa of Ávila. Others we may be meeting for the first time—Kateri Tekakwitha from America and Mary MacKillop from Australia.

On a personal note, I am pleased to see that so many fellow Benedictines have found their way into this book. The collection moves from St. Benedict to St. Anselm and down to Christian de Chergé, who was martyred in Algeria with his six companions in 1996.

They have very different stories to tell us, but the thread that binds them is a passionate love of God and a willingness to be still, to "waste time with God" (often in the midst of hectic lives) and allow God to love them. These men and women invite us to allow God to love us in the same way. They are not "different." Some may be canonized saints, but more important, they are our brothers and sisters, closer to us than we can imagine. They invite us into an intimacy with Father, Son, and Holy Spirit that we perhaps never dared to believe possible. They have much to teach us and to share with us. *The Book of Catholic Wisdom* is an introduction to some outstanding individuals who may become our lifelong friends.

— CARDINAL BASIL HUME (1923–99)
NINTH ARCHBISHOP OF WESTMINSTER

PREFACE

In bringing together examples of our remarkable spiritual heritage, it quickly becomes clear that there are many ways in which the "cake" can be cut. The material could certainly be dealt with in a strictly chronological fashion, but overall it has seemed more helpful to group passages thematically, maintaining the chronology within themes.

The publishers specifically requested that this book bring together writings from ancient and modern authors in communion with the bishop of Rome. The result has been an unfortunate neglect of the great writings of other traditions. If, however, I had been given a totally free hand in the selection of material, the anthology would never have been completed, and it would have been even more difficult to decide what to omit.

I did not originally intend to include the work of living writers, but this became difficult when compiling the section on marriage. Spiritual writing on the subject has made rapid strides over the past thirty years, and such improvement was long overdue! Two of the writers whose material appears in this section are therefore very much alive, and I thank William Johnston and Barbara Wood for allowing their work to be included.

In principle I had intended to use only direct quotations in this book. However, some of those I wished to include, such as Blessed Kateri Tekakwitha and the Korean martyrs, did not leave written testimony, and it nevertheless

seemed appropriate to include material that was illustrative
of their lives. In other cases I have included outstanding
biographical material despite the fact that the subject of
the piece left written testimony, e.g., Ronald Knox's vivid
portrait of St. Anselm and David Gibbs's moving description of the modern African martyr John Bradburne.

The list of Authors and Subjects includes all those
who appear in the text either in their own words or as the
subject of another author's work. Where the other authors
are of particular eminence they too have a short biographical entry (e.g., St. Adamnan writing about St. Columba).
With regard to dates and biographical details, I have gener-
ally been guided by the 1998 revision of the *Oxford Dic-
tionary of the Christian Church*.

If I have had a personal concern, it has been to choose
passages that counteract the unspoken assumption that God
is boring. Should childhood experience of religion have
consisted of hours spent listening to tedious and incomprehensible sermons, it is perhaps inevitable that the subject
of such homilies will seem boring. In *Best of Both Worlds* by
Bernard Basset, one of the characters accuses her learned
theologian son of the serious shortcoming of "making religion dull." Some readers may be familiar with Gerard W.
Hughes's book *God of Surprises* and its portrayal of Uncle
George—the elderly relative bent on hurling into the furnace of the damned those who fail to visit him once a week
or who act in other ways likely to displease him. "We observe what we are told are his wishes and dare not admit,
even to ourselves, that we loathe him."

If Uncle George is the God in whom we believe, a
healthy dose of agnosticism may put us on the road to being discovered by the "God of surprises"—the God who

shows a marked preference for those whose actions would have Uncle George lining them up for the furnace.

"Why does your Master eat with tax collectors and sinners?" asked the scribes and Pharisees of the disciples. Perhaps in part because sinners are better company than scribes and Pharisees. There seems little doubt that dubious characters reveled in the company of Jesus; otherwise they would not have kept inviting him to their parties.

This is the God whom the saints and mystics discover, the God who first discovers them. In *The Book of Catholic Wisdom,* passages from their writings are taken from the earliest centuries to the present day. Many of those included have died as martyrs—some of them very recently. While it is impossible to be accurate, it is widely believed that of the tens of thousands of martyrdoms suffered over the past two millennia, more than half have taken place during the past century.

I am in debt to those who have spent so much of their time advising and helping me with this collection. Although the final result inevitably reflects personal preference, I have tried to spread the net broadly by including material from many countries.

I am more in debt to those who have carried this undertaking in their prayers. The anthology is dedicated to them in the knowledge that the book would not have been completed without their support. The shortcomings are my own, and while every effort has been made to trace the source of each passage, these efforts have not always been successful. I ask the indulgence of those concerned and hope that they will get in touch with me so that appropriate acknowledgment may be made in any future edition.

ACKNOWLEDGMENTS

A very great debt is due to Prof. Donna Orsuto of the Gregorian University and David Dawson Vasquez of the Catholic University of America. I would also like to thank Herbert Alphonso, S.J.; Donna Orietta Doria Pamphilj; Michael McNulty, S.J.; Gerald O'Collins, S.J.; Rev. Gregory Mustaciuolo; and Nicholas Schofield.

I am indebted to the International Academy of Marital Spirituality (INTAMS) in Brussels and its director, Mrs. Aldegonde Brenninkmeijer-Werhahn. Also to Hans Storm and Elvira Roncalli of the Library for the Interdisciplinary Study of Marriage (LIBISMA); to Julia Archer, Helen Archer, Stratford Caldecott, Mary Corbett, and Angela Dunlea of Marriage Care; and to Peter Grimer, Edith Dominian, Hilary and Richard Grey, Prof. Mary Grey, Barbara Wood, and William Johnston, S.J.

I am very grateful to the Benedictine community of Stanbrook Abbey and particularly Dame Felicitas Corrigan, Dame Philippa Edwards, Dame Teresa Rodrigues, and Dame Margaret Truran. Dame Maria Boulding has very kindly allowed me to use her translation of *The Confessions of St. Augustine.*

The following have been unfailingly generous in sharing their wisdom: Fr. Bernard, O.Cart., of Parkminster; Fr. Robert Llewelyn; Fr. Iain Matthew, O.C.D.; Petrina Morris; Madeleine Judd; Mary Stewart; Sally Trench; Benedict Vanier, O.C.S.O.; Jean Vanier; and Dr. Thérèse Vanier.

I would also like to thank John Atkinson, librarian of the Franciscan Study Centre in Canterbury; Elizabeth Basset; Sr. M. Bernard, P.C.C; Jeanne Bisgood, C.B.E.; Sr. Pia Buxton, I.B.V.M.; Sr. Emmanuel Orchard, I.B.V.M.; Mr. George Bull; Michael Campbell-Johnston, S.J.; Justin Coo; Heather Craufurd; Rev. Douglas Dales, chaplain of Marlborough College; Paddy Daly of the Catholic Media Office in Glasgow; Canon John Devane; Sr. Pamela Dillon, O.P., of the Dominican Monastery of Langeac; Cynthia Donnelly of the Madonna House Community in Combermere; John Dove, S.J.; Sr. Emmanuelle, O.P., of the Dominican Monastery of Bouvines; Thomas More Eyston; Andrew Forshaw, O.P., of Blackfriars, Oxford; Dr. Esther de Waal; Shirley du Boulay; Jim Forest; David Gibbs, S.J.; Jane Gore-Booth; Francesca, countess of Gosford; Sr. Frances Teresa, O.S.C.; Win Harrison; Gerard Hughes, S.J.; Lord Hylton.

Thanks to Louis Jebb, Lady Helen Asquith, and Lord Oxford for kindly allowing me to use Hilaire Belloc's letter to Katharine Asquith. To Hon. William Jolliffe; Prof. Edwin Judge of Macquarie University, Sydney; Sr. M. Benedetta of the Sisters of St. Joseph of the Sacred Heart in Sydney; Dom Philip Jebb, O.S.B., and Dom Boniface Hill, O.S.B., of Downside Abbey; Mark Le Fanu, O.B.E., and the Society of Authors; Angela Lewis; Mr. Aidan Mackey of the Chesterton Study Centre; Sr. Frances Makower, R.S.C.J.; Sr. Eileen Coke, R.S.C.J.; Thomas M. McCoog, S.J.; Dom Donald McGlynn, O.C.S.O., abbot of Nunraw; Dom John Moakler, O.C.S.O., abbot of Mount St. Bernard; Brigid McEwen; June McAllister; Caroline Morson; Edward O'Connor, C.S.C., of the University of Notre Dame; Pat O'Leary of *The Irish Catholic;* Eileen O'Reilly of the Legion of Mary in Dublin; Sr. Susan Richert, provincial team leader of the Sisters of the Presentation of the Blessed Virgin Mary; Canon Timothy Russ; Dom Cyprian Smith, O.S.B., of Ampleforth Abbey; Kathryn Spink; Barbara Swanekamp; Sr. Diane Szarfinski, O.C.D.; Sr. Teresa Patricia and Sr. Cecilia of the Little Sisters of Jesus; Jenny Thom of Chichester Cathedral Visitors Office; Fr. Roland Walls; Sr. Benedicta Ward, S.L.G; and James Wicksteed.

Mrs. Joan Bond of the Catholic Central Library in London has never failed to trace a document or a source— no matter how obscure.

My debt to the Benedictine community of the Adorers of the Sacred Heart of Montmartre is very great, particularly to Mother Xavier McMonagle, Mother Edmund Campion, and Mother John Baptist.

My brother, Martin de Bertodano, and my sisters, Joanna Hylton and Isabel Scott, have given me unstinting help.

Morag Reeve has been the most helpful and supportive of editors. I am very grateful to her for inviting me to compile this anthology. Kate Webster kindly cleared the permissions. I am most grateful to her, to Helen Porter, and to all at Darton, Longman and Todd, especially Sandy Waldron, for meticulously copyediting the manuscript, and Sandie Boccacci, for designing the text of the first edition. I am very grateful to the late Cardinal Hume for writing the foreword.

FINDING THE ESSENCE: DIVINE AND HUMAN LOVE

At the center of all things is the boundless, inexhaustible love of God. God is love (1 John 4:16). God revealed this outstanding fact through the unwavering fidelity of the covenant with Israel, then through the coming of Jesus Christ, who extends the love of God to all. God's divine love contains the promise of salvation. It shines forth in Jesus' selfless act of laying down his life for his friends.

Human beings receive God's love and offer it back to God and to each other. Love is the standard by which all people will ultimately be judged—a high standard indeed, for we are commanded to love even our enemies. We can aspire to this standard because the very life of God dwells within us.

I

FATHER, SON, AND HOLY SPIRIT

When the Advocate comes whom I will send you from the Father, the Spirit of truth that proceeds from the Father, he will testify to me. And you also testify, because you have been with me from the beginning.

—JOHN 15:26–27

Like to God

Who is there who can hear the names of the Holy Spirit and not feel exaltation in his soul, not lift up his thoughts to that supreme nature? For he is called the Spirit of God, the Spirit of truth, who proceeds from the Father, the upright Spirit, the guiding Spirit. His chief and distinguishing name is Holy Spirit.

To the Spirit all creatures turn for their sanctification; all who live virtuously seek him and are, by his influence, refreshed and helped toward their own natural end. . . .

Even as bright and shining bodies, once touched by a ray of light falling on them, become even more glorious and themselves cast another light, so too souls that carry

3

the Spirit, and are enlightened by the Spirit, become spiritual themselves and send forth grace upon others.

This grace enables them to foresee the future, to understand mysteries, to grasp hidden things, to receive spiritual blessings, to have their thoughts fixed on heavenly things, and to dance with the angels. So is their joy unending, so is their perseverance in God unfailing, so do they acquire likeness to God, so—most sublime of all—do they themselves become divine.

— ST. BASIL THE GREAT (C. 330 –79)

Seek God by Faith

Who then is God? He is Father, Son, and Holy Spirit, one God. Seek no further concerning God, for those who wish to know the great deep must first review the natural world. For knowledge of the Trinity is properly likened to the depths of the sea, according to that saying of the Sage. And the great deep, who shall fathom it? Since, just as the depth of the sea is invisible to human sight, even so the godhead of the Trinity is found to be unknowable by human senses. And thus if, I say, a man wishes to know what he ought to believe, let him not think that he understands better by speech than by believing; because when he seeks it, knowledge of the godhead will recede farther than it was.

Therefore seek the supreme wisdom, not by verbal debate, but by the perfection of a good life, not with the tongue, but with the faith that issues from singleness of heart, not with that which is gathered from the guests of a learned irreligion. If then you seek the unutterable by discussion, he will fly farther from you than he was. If you

seek by faith, wisdom shall stand in her accustomed station
at the gate, and where she dwells she shall at least in part
be seen. But then is she also truly in some measure attained
when the invisible is believed in a manner that passes understanding, for God must be believed invisible as he is,
though he be partly seen by the pure heart.

— ST. COLUMBANUS (C. 543 – 615)

Father, Son, and Holy Spirit

To the Trinity be praise!
   God is music, God is life
   that nurtures every creature in its kind.
Our God is the song of the angel throng
   and the splendor of secret ways
   hid from all humankind,
But God our life is the life of all.

— ST. HILDEGARD OF BINGEN (1098 –1179)

The Holy Spirit Is Life

The Holy Spirit is life that gives life,
Moving all things.
It is the root in every creature
And purifies all things,
Wiping away sins,
Anointing wounds.

It is radiant life, worthy of praise,
Awakening and enlivening
All things.

— ST. HILDEGARD OF BINGEN (1098–1179)

The Love of the Trinity

For when two persons who mutually love embrace each other with supreme longing and take supreme delight in each other's love, then the supreme joy of the first is in intimate love of the second, and conversely the excellent joy of the second is in love of the first. As long as only the first is loved by the second, he alone seems to possess the delights of his excellent sweetness. Similarly, as long as the second does not have someone who shares in love for a third, he lacks the sharing of excellent joy. In order that both may be able to share delights of that kind, it is necessary for them to have someone who shares in love for a third.

When those who love mutually are of such great benevolence that, as we have said, they wish every perfection to be shared, then it is necessary, as has been said, that each with equal desire and for a similar reason seek out someone with whom to share love, and that each devotedly possess such a one, according to the fullness of his power.

———•———

When one person gives love to another and he alone loves only the other, there certainly is love, but it is not a shared love. When two love each other mutually and give to each

other the affection of supreme longing, when the affection
of the first goes out to the second and the affection of the
second goes out to the first and tends as it were in diverse
ways—in this case there certainly is love on both sides, but
it is not shared love. Shared love is properly said to exist
when a third person is loved by two persons harmoniously
and in community, and the affection of the two persons is
fused into one affection by the flame of love for the third.
From these things it is evident that shared love would have
no place in Divinity itself if a third person were lacking to
the other two persons. Here we are not speaking of just
any shared love but of supreme shared love—a shared love
of a sort such that a creature would never merit from the
Creator and for which it would never be found worthy.

— RICHARD OF ST. VICTOR (D. 1173)

Paradiso

O Light Eternal fixed in Self alone,
known only to Yourself, and knowing Self,
You love and glow, knowing and being known!

That circling which, as I conceived it, shone
In You as Your own first reflected light
when I had looked deep into It a while,

seemed in Itself and in Its own Self-color
to be depicted with man's very image.
My eyes were totally absorbed in It.

As the geometer who tries so hard
to square the circle, but cannot discover,
think as he may, the principle involved,

so did I strive with this new mystery:
I yearned to know how could our image fit
into the circle, how could it conform;

but my own wings could not take me so high—
then a great flash of understanding struck
my mind, and suddenly its wish was granted.

At this point power failed high fantasy
but, like a wheel in perfect balance turning,
I felt my will and my desire impelled
by the Love that moves the sun and the other stars.

— DANTE ALIGHIERI (1265 –1321)

God, Father and Mother

Jesus Christ, who does good to overcome evil, is our true
mother. We take our lives from him, which is the start of
motherhood, together with all the loving care that follows
on, without end.

As truly as God is our father, so, just as truly, God is
our mother. And he showed this in everything, especially
in those sweet words when he said:

"It is I." That is to say,
"It is I, the strength and goodness of fatherhood.
It is I, the wisdom of motherhood.
It is I, the light and grace of holy love.
It is I, the Trinity.
It is I, the unity.
I am the sovereign goodness in all things.
It is I who teach you to love.
It is I who teach you to desire.

It is I who am the lasting fulfillment of all true
desires."

—JULIAN OF NORWICH (C. 1342 – C. 1420)

Eternal Trinity

O eternal Trinity, eternal godhead! This godhead, your divine nature, made immensely precious the blood of the
only-begotten Son. Eternal Trinity, you are like a deep sea,
in which the more I seek, the more I find; and the more I
find, the more I seek you. You fill the soul, yet somehow
without satisfying it: in the abyss that you are, you so fill
the soul that it ever continues to hunger and thirst for you,
desiring you, eager in your light to see you, who are the
light.

With the light of my understanding, in your light I
have tasted and seen the abyss that you are, eternal Trinity,
and the beauty of your creation. Then looking at myself in
you, I have seen that I am your image; this is a gift that I
receive from you in your power, eternal Father, and in your
wisdom, which is attributed to your only-begotten Son.
The Holy Spirit who proceeds from you, Father, and from
your Son has prepared me, giving me a will to love you.

———•———

Eternal Trinity, you are the Creator, I the creature. I have
come to know, in the new creation you made of me in the
blood of your Son, that you are in love with the beauty of
your creature.

O eternal Trinity, God, you are an abyss, a deep sea;
you have given yourself to me—what greater could you

give? You are a fire, ever burning and never consumed, consuming in your heat all the self-love of the soul, taking away all coldness. By your light you enlighten our minds, as by your light you have brought me to know your truth.

In this light I know you, and I picture you to myself as the supreme good, the good beyond all good, the blessed good, the incomprehensible good, the inestimable good, beauty beyond all beauty, wisdom beyond all wisdom. You are wisdom itself. You are the food of angels, who gave yourself to men in the fire of your love.

You are the garment that covers every nakedness. You feed the hungry in your sweetness, because you are gentle, without a trace of bitterness. O eternal Trinity!

— ST. CATHERINE OF SIENA (C.1347–80)

Trinity, Whom I Adore

O my God, Trinity whom I adore, help me to forget myself entirely so as to be established in you, as changeless and calm as if my soul were already in eternity. May nothing disturb my peace or draw me forth from you, O my Unchanging Lord, but may every minute carry me further into the depths of your Mystery. Calm my soul; make of it your heaven, your beloved abode and the place of your rest. May I never leave you alone there, but may I be there entirely, wholly awake in my faith, all adoring and wholly yielded up to your creative action.

O my beloved Christ, crucified by love! I want to be a bride for your heart; I want to cover you in glory and love you—until I die of it! But I feel how powerless I am, and I ask you to "clothe me with yourself," to identify my soul with all the movements of your soul, to immerse me in yourself, to take possession of me, to substitute yourself for me so that my life may be but a radiance of your Life. Come into me as Adorer, as Restorer, and as Savior.

—— • ——

O eternal Word, Utterance of my God, I wish to spend my life listening to you; I wish to make myself wholly teachable so as to learn everything from you. Then through all nights, all voids, all powerlessness, I wish to keep my eyes always upon you and live beneath your great light. O my beloved Star, fascinate me so that I may no longer be able to withdraw from your radiance.

O consuming Fire, Spirit of love, "come upon me" so that there may be brought about in my soul a kind of incarnation of the Word: that I may be for him an additional humanity in which he renews the whole of his Mystery.

And you, O Father, bend down toward your poor little creature, "overshadow" her, see in her only "the Beloved in whom you are well pleased."

O my Three, my All, my Beatitude, infinite Solitude, Immensity in which I lose myself, I yield myself to you as a prey. Bury yourself in me that I may bury myself in you, until I depart to contemplate in your light the abyss of your splendors.

— BLESSED ELIZABETH OF THE TRINITY
(1880–1906)

GOD'S LOVE FOR US

As the Father loves me, so I also love you. Remain in my love. If you keep my commandments, you will remain in my love, just as I have kept my Father's commandments and remain in his love. I have told you this so that my joy may be in you and your joy may be complete. This is my commandment: love one another as I love you.

—JOHN 15:9–12

Your Life for My Salvation

Where do you pasture your flock, O good shepherd, you who take on your shoulders the whole flock, for the whole of human nature that you take on your shoulders forms one sheep. Show me the place of green pastures and the restful waters, lead me to the grass that nourishes, call me by name, so that I who am your sheep may hear your voice. Give me by your voice eternal life. Speak to me, you whom my soul loves.

This is how I name you, for your name is above every name and cannot be uttered or comprehended by any rational nature. Your name, which reveals your goodness, is the love my soul has for you. How can I not love you who loved me, even though I was black, so much that you laid down your life for the sheep whose shepherd you are? Greater love than this cannot be conceived, that you should purchase my salvation with your life.

— ST. GREGORY OF NYSSA (C. 335 – C. 395)

The Ever Adorable Trinity

Her most loving Jesus seemed to draw her toward himself by the breath of love of his pierced heart, and to wash her in the water flowing from it, and then to sprinkle her with the life-giving blood of his heart (cf. John 19:34). With this action she began to revive, and from the smallest cinder she was invigorated and grew into a green tree, whose branches were divided in three, in the form of a fleur-de-lis. Then the Son of God took this tree and presented it with gratitude to the glory of the ever adorable Trinity. When he had presented it, the whole blessed Trinity with great graciousness bowed down toward the offering. God the Father, in his divine omnipotence, set in the upper branches all the fruit that this soul would have been able to produce, were she to correspond aright to divine omnipotence. In the same way, she saw the Son of God and the Holy Spirit setting in the other two sections of the branches the fruits of wisdom and goodness.

—•—

When she had received the body of Christ, she beheld her soul . . . in the likeness of a tree fixing its roots in the wound of the side of Jesus Christ; she felt in some new and marvelous way that there was passing through this wound, as through a root, and penetrating into all her branches and fruit and leaves a wondrous sap that was the virtue of the humanity and divinity of Jesus Christ. Thus, through her soul, the work of his whole life took on more splendor, like gold gleaming through crystal. Hereupon not only the blessed Trinity, but all the saints, rejoiced with delight and wonder. They all rose up in reverence and, as though on bended knee, offered their merits, represented like crowns, hanging them on the branches of the tree we have mentioned, to the praise and honor of him the splendor of whose glory now shone through her and gladdened them with fresh delight.

—ST. GERTRUDE THE GREAT (C. 1256 – C. 1302)

The Hazelnut

At this time our Lord showed me an inward sight of his homely loving. I saw that he is everything that is good and comforting to us. He is our clothing. In his love he wraps and holds us. He enfolds us in love, and he will never let us go.

And then he showed me a little thing, the size of a hazelnut, in the palm of my hand—and it was as round as a ball. I looked at it with my mind's eye and I thought: "What can this be?" and answer came: "It is all that is made." I marveled that it could last, for I thought it might have crumbled to nothing, it was so small. And the answer came into my mind: "It lasts, and ever shall, because God loves it." And so all things have being through the love of God.

In this little thing I saw three truths. The first is that
God made it. The second is that God loves it. And the third
is that God looks after it.

——— • ———

From the time it was shown, I often asked to know what
was our Lord's meaning. And fifteen years after, and more,
I was answered in inward understanding, saying this:

"Would you know your Lord's meaning in this?
Learn it well.
Love was his meaning.
Who showed it you? Love.
What did he show you? Love.
Why did he show you? For love.
Hold fast to this and you shall learn and know more
   about love, but you shall never know nor learn about
   anything except love forever."

So was I taught that love was our Lord's meaning.
And I saw full surely that before ever God made us,
   he loved us. And this love was never quenched,
   nor ever shall be.
And in this love he has done all his works.
And in this love he has made all things profitable to us.
And in this love our life is everlasting.
In our making we had beginning, but the love in which
   he made us was in him from without beginning.
In which love we have our beginning.
And all this shall we see in God without end—which
   Jesus grant us.

—JULIAN OF NORWICH (C. 1342 – C. 1420)

You Gave Us Memory

You drew us out of your holy mind
like a flower
petaled with our soul's three powers,
and into each power
you put the whole plant,
so that they might bear fruit in your garden,
might come back to you
with the fruit you gave them.
And you would come back to the soul
to fill her with your blessedness.
There the soul dwells—
like the fish in the sea
and the sea in the fish.
You gave us memory
so that we might be able to hold your blessings
and so bring forth the flower of glory to your name
and the fruit of profit to ourselves.
You gave us understanding
to understand your truth
and your will—
your will that wants only that we be made holy—
so that we might bear first the flower of glory
and then the fruit of virtue.
And you gave us our will
so that we might be able to love
what our understanding has seen
and what our memory has held.

— ST. CATHERINE OF SIENA (C.1347–80)

Living Flame

Flame, alive, compelling,
yet tender past all telling,
reaching the secret center of my soul!
Since now evasion's over,
finish your work, my Lover,
break the last thread, wound me and make me whole!

> Burn that is for my healing!
> Wound of delight past feeling!
> Ah, gentle hand whose touch is a caress,
> foretaste of heaven conveying
> and every debt repaying:
> slaying, you give me life for death's distress.

O lamps of fire bright-burning
with splendid brilliance, turning
deep caverns of my soul to pools of light!
Once shadowed, dim, unknowing,
now their strange newfound glowing
gives warmth and radiance for my Love's delight.

> Ah! gentle and so loving
> you wake within me, proving
> that you are there in secret and alone;
> your fragrant breathing stills me,
> your grace, your glory fills me
> so tenderly your love becomes my own.

— ST. JOHN OF THE CROSS (1542–91)

Aware of God's Presence

By the supernatural virtue of Charity, Divine Love dwells
in the soul and in a very personal, intimate relationship, for
there are several different ways in which God can be present. First of all, God is present everywhere in the world,
because He is the Power that made the world, the Wisdom
that planned it, and the Love that executed it. God is also
present—but personally—in the Eucharist, and in our
souls so long as the Sacramental presence lasts. But there is
still another Divine presence that is more abiding, and that
is the presence of God in the soul through Charity. To be
in the state of Grace through Charity does not mean that
we have something, but that we are something. For one of
the consequences of the Faith is that an extraordinary
event happens to us: we receive a Gift. Many baptized souls
are ignorant of this mystery, and remain ignorant of it
throughout their lives; for just as it is possible for some
families to live under the same roof and never communicate, so it is also possible for a man to have God in his soul
and yet hold little intimate exchange with Him. The more
holy souls become, and the more detached from the world,
the greater their consciousness of God's presence.

— FULTON SHEEN (1895–1979)

OUR LOVE FOR GOD

When they had finished breakfast, Jesus said to Simon Peter, "Simon, son of John, do you love me more than these?" He said to him, "Yes, Lord, you know that I love you." He said to him, "Feed my lambs." He then said to him a second time, "Simon, son of John, do you love me?" He said to him, "Yes, Lord, you know that I love you." He said to him, "Tend my sheep." He said to him the third time, "Simon, son of John, do you love me?" Peter was distressed that he had said to him a third time, "Do you love me?" and he said to him, "Lord, you know everything; you know that I love you." [Jesus] said to him, "Feed my sheep."

—JOHN 21:15–17

The Beauty of God

Having received a commandment—to love God—we possess the power to love implanted in us at the moment we were constituted. The proof of this is not external, but anyone can learn it from himself and within himself. For by nature we desire beautiful things though we differ as to what is supremely beautiful, and without being taught, we have affection toward those near and dear to us, and we spontaneously show goodwill to all our benefactors.

Now what is more marvelous than the divine beauty? What thought has more charm than the magnificence of God? What yearning of the soul is so keen and intolerable as that which comes from God upon the soul that is cleansed from all evil and cries with true affection: "I am wounded with love"? Ineffable wholly and inexplicable are the flashes of the divine beauty.

— ST. BASIL THE GREAT (C. 330–79)

Late Have I Loved You

Late have I loved you, Beauty so ancient and so new,
late have I loved you!
Lo, you were within,
but I outside, seeking there for you,
and upon the shapely things you have made I rushed
   headlong,
I, misshapen.
You were with me, but I was not with you.
They held me back far from you,
those things which would have no being
were they not in you.
You called, shouted, broke through my deafness;
you flared, blazed, banished my blindness;
you lavished your fragrance, I gasped, and now I pant
   for you;

I tasted you, and I hunger and thirst;
you touched me, and I burned for your peace.

— ST. AUGUSTINE OF HIPPO (354 – 430)

Possess My Heart

"Set me as a seal on your heart." As though to say: Love
me, as I love you; have me in your mind, in your memory,
in your desire; in your sighing, your groaning, your weeping. Remember, man, in what state I fashioned you, how
far I preferred you before the rest of creatures, the dignity
with which I ennobled you; how I crowned you with
glory and honor, made you a little less than the angels, and
subjected all things under your feet. Remember not only
the great things I did for you, but what harsh indignities I
bore on your behalf, and see if you are not acting wickedly
against me, if you do not love me. For who loves you as I
love you? Who created you, if not I? Who redeemed you,
if not I?

Lord, take away from me the heart of stone, a heart
shrunken and uncircumcised—take it away and give me a
new heart, a heart of flesh, a clean heart. You cleanse our
heart and love the heart that is clean—possess my heart
and dwell in it, both holding it and filling it. You surpass
what is highest in me, and yet are within my inmost self!
Pattern of beauty and seal of holiness, mold my heart in
your likeness: mold my heart under your mercy, God of my
heart and God my portion forever.

— BALDWIN OF CANTERBURY (D. 1190)

The Fountain of Life

Arise, then, bride of Christ, be like the dove that nests in the rock face at the mouth of a cavern, and there, like a sparrow that finds its home, do not cease to keep vigil; there, like a turtledove, hide the fledglings of your chaste love; place your lips there to draw water from the wells of your Savior. For this is the spring flowing from the middle of paradise; it divides and becomes four rivers, then spreads through all devout hearts, and waters the whole world and makes it fruitful.

O soul devoted to God, whoever you may be, run to this source of life and light with eager longing. And with the power of your inmost heart cry out to him: "O indescribable beauty of God most high! O pure radiance of everlasting light! O life that gives life to all life! O light that illuminates every light, and preserves in its undying splendor the myriad flames that have shone before the throne of your godhead from the dawn of time!

"O water eternal and inaccessible, clear and sweet, flowing from the spring that is hidden from the eyes of all mortal men; the spring whose depths cannot be plumbed, whose height cannot be measured, whose shores cannot be charted, whose purity cannot be muddied."

From this source flows the river that makes glad the city of God, so that with glad shouts and songs of thanksgiving we sing to you our hymns of praise, and by experience prove that with you is the fountain of life, and in your light we shall see light.

— ST. BONAVENTURE (C. 1217–74)

Not Counting the Cost

Teach us, good Lord, to serve Thee
as Thou deservest,
to give and not to count the cost;
to fight and not to heed the wounds;
to toil and not to seek for rest;
to labor and not to ask for any reward
save that of knowing that we do Thy will.

— ATTRIBUTED TO ST. IGNATIUS OF LOYOLA
(1491–1556)

Thy Love and Thy Grace

Take, Lord, and receive all my liberty,
my memory, my understanding, and my entire will,
all that I have and possess.
Thou hast given all to me.
To Thee, O Lord, I return it.
All is Thine, dispose of it wholly according to Thy will.
Give me Thy love and Thy grace,
for this is sufficient for me.

— ST. IGNATIUS OF LOYOLA (1491–1556)

God Alone

The more God gives, the more he makes us desire, until we
are empty and he is able to fill us with good things.

The immense benefits of God can only be contained
by empty and solitary hearts. Therefore our Lord, who

loves you greatly, wishes you to be quite alone, for he desires to be your only companion.

You must needs apply your mind to him alone, and in him alone content yourself, that in him you may find all consolation. Although God is always with us, if we set our hearts on other things beside him we cannot be at peace.

God knows what is best for all and orders affairs for our good. Think on this only, that all is ordained by God. And pour in love where there is no love, and you will draw love out.

— ST. JOHN OF THE CROSS (1542 – 91)

Prayer of Abandonment

Father,
I abandon myself into your hands,
do with me what you will.
Whatever you may do, I thank you:
I am ready for all, I accept all.
Let only your will be done in me
and in all your creatures.
I wish no more than this, O Lord.
Into your hands, I commend my soul;
I offer it to you
with all the love of my heart;
for I love you, Lord,
and so need to give myself:

to surrender myself into your hands
without reserve and with boundless confidence:
for you are my father.

— CHARLES DE FOUCAULD (1858–1916)

God's Love Brings Joy

The love of the Lord is greater in realization than in desire. Here, it differs from worldly love, which is greater in
anticipation than in realization. All the popular love songs
tell us: "How happy we will be!" Divine love, on the contrary, does not look at all enchanting or ecstatic before we
have it: the Cross frightens us; the sacrifice of selfishness
and sin seems like a little death; non-sensual love appears
as lovelessness. But after one makes the surrender, gives up
the field to win the pearl, then one is possessed of a joy that
is ineffable, that beggars all description. The discovery makes
a man act so differently that his friends think he has lost his
mind, but actually, he has found his soul, which the believer would not now give up for anything in all the world.

— FULTON SHEEN (1895–1979)

Self-Surrender

Being in love with God, as experienced, is being in love in
an unrestricted fashion. All love is self-surrender, but being
in love with God is being in love without limits or quali-
fications or conditions or reservations. Just as unrestricted
questioning is our capacity for self-transcendence, so being

in love in an unrestricted fashion is the proper fulfillment of that capacity.

That fulfillment is not the product of our knowledge and choice. On the contrary, it dismantles and abolishes the horizon in which our knowing and choosing went on, and it sets up a new horizon in which the love of God will transvalue our values and the eyes of that love will transform our knowing.

Though not the product of our knowing and choosing, it is a conscious dynamic state of love, joy, peace, which manifests itself in acts of kindness, goodness, fidelity, gentleness, and self-control (Galatians 5:22).

— BERNARD LONERGAN (1904 – 84)

Known by Jesus

What does it mean to be known by Jesus? It means accepting that all should be unveiled, in full light, in his sight and before our own eyes: our weaknesses and limits, and the whole sum of infidelities, great and small, that constitute our existence. Even though, by the mercy of God, we may not be great sinners, nevertheless there are all sorts of things in our lives that we find it difficult to look at honestly. Immediately after committing a fault, especially, we are sometimes extremely unwilling to acknowledge in the presence of Jesus, honestly and frankly, and without masks, that we are no more than what we are. That is why we are afraid of the light.

Think, for example, of the story of the woman taken in adultery. Jesus simply says to her accusers: "Let him who is without sin among you be the first to throw a stone at

her" (John 8:7). And one after another, all of them flee
from his sight. They run far away from him. The only one
who remains in the presence of the Lord is the woman accused who has now become the woman forgiven, in the
light, because she hid nothing of her poverty from him. This
is the deepest secret of an intimate relationship with the
Lord: we have to allow him to look at us unreservedly, even
if his gaze seems indiscreet, for in reality it is overflowing
with mercy alone.

— A CARTHUSIAN

LOVE OF NEIGHBOR

Then the king will say to those on his right, "Come, you who are blessed by my Father. Inherit the kingdom prepared for you from the foundation of the world. For I was hungry and you gave me food, I was thirsty and you gave me drink, a stranger and you welcomed me, naked and you clothed me, ill and you cared for me, in prison and you visited me." Then the righteous will answer him and say, "Lord, when did we see you hungry and feed you, or thirsty and give you drink? When did we see you a stranger and welcome you, or naked and clothe you? When did we see you ill or in prison, and visit you?"

—MATTHEW 25:34–39

Give to the Poor

Would you honor the body of Christ? Do not despise his nakedness; do not honor him here in church clothed in silk vestments and then pass him by unclothed and frozen outside. Remember that he who said, "This is my body," and made good his words, also said, "You saw me hungry and gave me no food," and, "in so far as you did it not to one of these, you did it not to me." In the first sense the body of Christ does not need clothing but worship from a pure heart. In the second sense it does need clothing and all the care we can give it.

We must learn to be discerning Christians and to honor Christ in the way in which he wants to be honored. It is only right that honor given to anyone should take the form most acceptable to the recipient, not to the giver. Peter thought he was honoring the Lord when he tried to stop him washing his feet, but this was far from being genuine homage. So give God the honor he asks for, that is, give your money generously to the poor. God has no need of golden vessels but of golden hearts.

I am not saying you should not give golden altar vessels and so on, but I am insisting that nothing can take the place of almsgiving. The Lord will not refuse to accept the first kind of gift, but he prefers the second, and quite naturally, because in the first case only the donor benefits, in the second case the poor get the benefit. The gift of a chalice may be ostentatious; almsgiving is pure benevolence.

———— • ————

What is the use of loading Christ's table with gold cups while he himself is starving? Feed the hungry, and then if you have any money left over, spend it on the altar table. Will you make a cup of gold and withhold a cup of water? What use is it to adorn the altar with cloth of gold hangings and deny Christ a coat for his back! What would that profit you? Tell me: if you saw someone starving and refused to give him any food but instead spent your money on adorning the altar with gold, would he thank you? Would he not rather be outraged? Or if you saw someone

in rags and stiff with cold and then did not give him clothing but set up golden columns in his honor, would he not
say he was being made a fool of and insulted?

Consider that Christ is that tramp who comes in
need of a night's lodging. You turn him away and then start
laying rugs on the floor, draping the walls, hanging lamps
on silver chains on the columns. Meanwhile the tramp is
locked up in prison, and you never give him a glance. Well,
again, I am not condemning munificence in these matters.
Make your house beautiful by all means but also look after
the poor, or rather look after the poor first. No one was
ever condemned for not adorning his house, but those
who neglect the poor were threatened with hellfire for all
eternity and a life of torment with devils. Adorn your
house if you will, but do not forget your brother in distress.
He is a temple of infinitely greater value.

— ST. JOHN CHRYSOSTOM (C. 349 – 407)

Love Your Neighbor

You do not yet see God, but by loving your neighbor you
gain the sight of God; by loving your neighbor you purify
your eye for seeing God, as John says clearly: "If you do not
love the brother whom you see, how will you be able to
love God whom you do not see?"

You are told: love God. If you say to me: "Show me
the one I am to love," what shall I answer, except what
John himself says: "No one has ever seen God"? Do not
think that you are altogether unsuited to seeing God—no,
for John states: "God is love, and he who dwells in love
is dwelling in God." Love your neighbor therefore, and

observe the source of that love in you; there, as best you can, you will see God.

So then, begin to love your neighbor. "Share your bread with the hungry, and bring the homeless poor into your house; if you see the naked, cover him, and do not despise the servants of your kinsfolk."

If you do this, what will you obtain? "Then shall your light break forth like the morning." Your light is your God; to you he is "morning light," because he will come to you after the night of the world; he neither rises nor sets, because he abides always.

By loving your neighbor and being concerned about your neighbor, you make progress on your journey. Where is your journey, if not to the Lord God, to him whom we must love with all our heart, and with all our soul, and with all our mind? We have not yet reached the Lord, but we have our neighbor with us. So then, support him with whom you are traveling so that you may come to him with whom you long to dwell.

— ST. AUGUSTINE OF HIPPO (354 – 430)

Love Manifested in Us

There are two kinds of mercy then, mercy on earth and mercy in heaven, human mercy and divine mercy. What is human mercy like? It makes you concerned for the hardship of the poor. What is divine mercy like? It forgives sinners. Whatever generosity human mercy shows during our life on earth, divine mercy repays when we reach our fatherland. In this world God is cold and hungry in all the poor, as he himself said: "As you did it to one of the least of these my brethren, you did it to me." God then is pleased to give from heaven, but he desires to receive on earth.

What sort of people are we—when God gives, we want to receive, when he asks, we refuse to give? When a poor man is hungry, Christ is in need, as he said himself: "I was hungry and you gave me no food." Take care not to despise the hardship of the poor, if you would hope, without fear, to have your sins forgiven. My dear brethren, Christ is now hungry, he is hungry and thirsty in all the poor; and what he receives on earth he returns in heaven.

I put you this question, dearly beloved: what is it you want, what is it you are looking for, when you come to church? What indeed if not mercy? Show mercy on earth, and you will receive mercy in heaven. A poor man is begging from you, and you are begging from God: he asks for a scrap, you ask for eternal life. Give to the beggar, so that you may deserve to receive from Christ. Listen to his words: "Give and it shall be given you." What effrontery it is for you to want to receive what you refuse to give! And so when you come to church, give whatever alms you can to the poor in accordance with your means.

— ST. CAESARIUS OF ARLES (C. 470 – 542)

St. Francis of Assisi's Kiss

The lover of complete humility went to the lepers and lived with them, serving them all most diligently for God's sake. He washed their feet, bandaged their ulcers, drew the pus from their wounds, and washed out the diseased matter; he even kissed their ulcerous wounds out of his remarkable devotion, he who was soon to be a physician of the gospel. As a result, he received such power from the Lord that he had miraculous effectiveness in healing spiritual and physical illnesses. I will cite one case among many, which occurred after the fame of the man of God became more widely known. There was a man in the vicinity of Spoleto whose mouth and cheek were being eaten away by a certain horrible disease. He could not be helped by any medical treatment and went on a pilgrimage to implore the intercession of the holy apostles. On his way back from visiting their shrines, he happened to meet God's servant. When out of devotion he wanted to kiss Francis's footprints, that humble man, refusing to allow it, kissed the mouth of the one who wished to kiss his feet. In his remarkable compassion Francis, the servant of lepers, touched that horrible sore with his holy mouth, and suddenly every sign of the disease vanished and the sick man recovered the health he longed for. I do not know which of these we should admire more: the depth of his humility in such a compassionate kiss or his extraordinary power in such an amazing miracle.

(St. Francis of Assisi: c. 1181–1226)

— ST. BONAVENTURE (C. 1217–74)

A Vessel of God's Love

Oh my very dear and cherished son, I want you to imitate this Word who is our rule, and the saints who followed him. Then you will become one with him and will have a share in his greatheartedness to replace [your own] smallheartedness. I tell you again, unless you rise up, open your eyes, and take as your model the boundless goodness and love God has shown to his creatures, you will never attain such perfect greatness of soul but will be so smallhearted that you will have no room either for yourself or for your neighbors. This is why I want you, as I said, to be engulfed and set on fire in him, constantly gazing into the gentle eye of his charity, for then you will love perfectly what he loves, and hate what he hates. Lift up, lift up your puny heart, your small disordered conscience! Don't give any leverage to the wicked devil, who wants to prevent so much good and doesn't want to be thrown out of his city. No, I want you, with courageous heart and perfect zeal, to realize that the Holy Spirit's law is quite different from ours. Imitate that dear Paul, who was so in love, and be a vessel of affection that bears and proclaims the name of Jesus. It seems to me that Paul gazed into this eye and lost himself in it. And he was granted such a great soul that he was willing and even desired to be separated from God, an outcast, for the sake of his brothers and sisters. Paul was in love with whatever God was in love with. He saw that charity is never scandalized, is never confounded.

— ST. CATHERINE OF SIENA (C.1347– 80)

Be Cordial to Others

So far as you can without offending God, try to be genial and to behave in such a way with those you have to deal with that they may take pleasure in your conversation and may wish to imitate your life and manners, instead of being frightened and deterred from virtue.

The more holy someone is, the more cordial should they be with others.

Although you may be pained because their conversation is not what you would wish, never keep aloof if you want to help them and win their love.

Try to think rightly about God, sisters. He does not look at such trifling matters as you suppose; do not alarm your soul or lose courage, for you might lose greatly. Keep a pure intention and a firm resolve not to offend God, as I said, but do not trammel your soul, for instead of advancing in sanctity you would contract a number of imperfections and would not help others as you might have done.

— ST. TERESA OF ÁVILA (1515–82)

The Poor as God's Children

We should not judge the poor by their clothes and their outward appearance nor by their mental capacity, since they are often ignorant and uncouth. On the contrary, if you consider the poor in the light of faith, then you will see that they take the place of God the Son, who chose to be poor. Indeed, in his passion, having lost even the appearance of man, foolishness to the Gentiles and a scandal to the Jews, he showed he was to preach the gospel to the poor in these words: "He has sent me to preach good news to the poor." Therefore we should be of the same mind and should imitate what Christ did, caring for the poor, consoling them, helping them, and guiding them.

Christ chose to be born in poverty and took poor men as his disciples; he himself became the servant of the poor and so shared their condition that whatever good or harm was done to the poor, he said he would consider done to himself. Since God loves the poor, he also loves the lovers of the poor: when someone loves another, he loves too those who love or serve that other. So we too hope that God will love us on account of the poor. We visit them then; we strive to concern ourselves with the weak and the needy; we so share their sufferings that with the apostle we feel we have become all things to all men. Therefore we must strive to be deeply involved in the cares and sorrows of our neighbor and pray to God to inspire us with compassion and pity, filling our hearts and keeping them full.

— ST. VINCENT DE PAUL (C. 1580 –1660)

Give Yourself to the Present

To escape the distress caused by regret for the past or fear about the future, this is the rule to follow: leave the past to the infinite mercy of God, the future to his good providence; give the present wholly to his love by being faithful to his grace.

When God in his goodness sends you some disappointment, one of those trials that used to annoy you so much, before everything thank him for it as for a great favor all the more useful for the great work of your perfection in that it completely overturns the work of the moment.

Try, in spite of interior dislike, to show a kind face to troublesome people or to those who come to chatter about their troubles; leave at once prayer, reading, choir Office, in fact anything, to go where Providence calls you; and do what is asked of you quietly, peacefully, without hurry, and without vexation.

Should you fail in any of these points, make immediately an act of interior humility—not that sort of humility full of uneasiness and irritation against which St. Francis de Sales said so much, but a humility that is gentle, peaceful, and sweet.

—JEAN-PIERRE DE CAUSSADE (1675–1751)

Leper with the Lepers

Picture to yourself a collection of huts with eight hundred lepers. No doctor; in fact, as there is no cure there seems no place for a doctor's skill. A white man, who is a leper, and your humble servant do all the doctoring work.

Every morning, then, after my Mass, which is followed by an instruction, I go to visit the sick, half of whom are Catholics. On entering each hut, I begin by offering to hear their confession. Those who refuse this spiritual help are not, therefore, refused temporal assistance, which is given to all without distinction. Consequently, everyone, with the exception of a very few bigoted heretics, looks on me as a father. As for me, I make myself a leper with the lepers, to gain all to Jesus Christ. That is why, in preaching, I say we lepers, not my brethren, as in Europe. . . .

The average of deaths is about one every day. Many are so destitute that there is nothing to defray their burial expenses. They are simply wrapped in a blanket. As far as my duties allow me time, I make coffins myself for these poor people.

—BLESSED JOSEPH DE VEUSTER (FATHER DAMIEN OF MOLOKAI, 1840–89)

Likes and Dislikes

In the Gospel the Lord showed me clearly what his new commandment demands. I read in St. Matthew: "You have heard it said that you should love your neighbor and hate your enemy; but I say to you, love your enemies and pray for those who persecute you."

We all have our natural likes and dislikes. We may feel more drawn to one person and may be tempted to go a long way around to avoid meeting another. Well, the Lord tells me that the latter is the one I must love and pray for, even though the manner shown me leads me to believe that the person does not care for me. "If you love those that love you, what thanks are due to you? For sinners also love those who love them" (Luke 6:32).

Nor is it enough to love. We must prove our love. We take a natural delight in pleasing friends, but that is not love; even sinners do the same.

— ST. THÉRÈSE OF LISIEUX (1873 – 97)

Learning about Love

Early one morning on the steps of Precious Blood Church, a woman with cancer of the face was begging (beggars are allowed only in the slums) and when I gave her money (no sacrifice on my part but merely passing on alms which someone had given me) she tried to kiss my hand. The only thing I could do was kiss her dirty old face with the gaping hole in it where an eye and a nose had been. It sounds like a heroic deed but it was not. One gets used to ugliness so quickly. What we avert our eyes from one day is easily borne the next when we have learned a little more about love. Nurses know this, and so do mothers.

— DOROTHY DAY (1897–1980)

The Final Word Is Love

The final word is love. At times it has been, in the words of Father Zossima, a harsh and dreadful thing, and our very faith in love has been tried through fire.

We cannot love God unless we love each other, and to love we must know each other. We know him in the breaking of bread, and we know each other in the breaking of bread, and we are not alone anymore. Heaven is a banquet and life is a banquet, too, even with a crust, where there is companionship.

We have all known the long loneliness and we have learned that the only solution is love and that love comes with community.

— DOROTHY DAY (1897–1980)

John Bradburne's Wheelbarrow

At Mtemwa leper colony outside Harare, John Bradburne visited every leper every day just to make sure that all was well. If anybody needed any help, John was there to give it. He would bathe those who needed bathing, build fires, make beds, change dressings, and give out whatever he had received or bought for his people. At the beginning of the "round" his wheelbarrow was always full—full of sugar,

tea, sweets, onions, vegetables, nuts, tomatoes, bread, meat—
anything he had to give out. By the time he reached the
chapel for the midday Angelus, the barrow was empty, and
each leper had been helped in some small way.

After a period of quiet in the presence of the Lord,
the afternoon would be spent in much the same way—
cutting firewood, cleaning out the cattle grid, collecting
reeds for making hats, making tea or coffee for the sick, or
just popping in. . . .

Sometimes he would simply crouch on his haunches
and chatter away, trying to help and encourage.

At a death John was always present to give comfort to
the dying and to all the lepers who were losing a dear
friend. In a small community like Mtemwa, a death affects
everybody very deeply, and John helped the lepers, even
those who had no beliefs, to see that death was, in most
cases, a blessed relief from many years of suffering and the
opening of the door to joy, peace, and happiness.

(John Bradburne: 1921–79)

— FATHER DAVID GIBBS

SEEING THE CONNECTION: CREATION AND REDEMPTION

Creation and redemption are intimately linked. God's creation of all things ex nihilo— "out of nothing"—and Christ's work to redeem humanity are two aspects of one divine plan. The New Testament sees Christ as an active agent in creation: "For in him were created all things in heaven and on earth" (Col. 1:16).

Some theologians speak of the redemption as beginning with the life of Christ. But the church commonly describes it as a renewal of creation, as present in the beginning of things and active throughout history. Says the French theologian Teilhard de Chardin, "The prodigious expanses of time that preceded the first Christmas were not empty of Christ: they were imbued with the influx of his power." The redemption, then, is something intended not just for humanity but for the entire cosmos.

GOD THE CREATOR

*W*hen he established the heavens I was there,
    when he marked out the vault over the
  face of the deep;
When he made firm the skies above,
    when he fixed fast the foundations of the earth;
When he set for the sea its limit,
    so that the waters should not transgress his
    command;
Then was I beside him as his craftsman,
    and I was his delight day by day,
Playing before him all the while,
    playing on the surface of his earth;
    and I found delight in the sons of men.

—PROVERBS 8:27–31

Halcyon Days

The halcyon is a seabird that nests by the shore, laying its eggs in the sand, and bringing forth its young in the middle of winter when the sea beats against the land in violent and frequent storms. But during the seven days while the halcyon broods—for it takes but seven days to hatch its

43

young—all winds sink to rest, and the sea grows calm. And as it then is in need of food for its young ones, the most bountiful God grants this little creature another seven days of calm: that it may feed its young. Since all sailors know of this, they give this time the name of the *halcyon days.*

These things are ordered by the Providence of God for the creatures that are without reason, that you may be led to seek of God the things you need for your salvation. And when for this small bird he holds back the great and fearful sea, and bids it be calm in winter, what will he not do for you made in his own image? And if he should so tenderly cherish the halcyon, how much more will he not give you, when you call upon him with all your heart?

— ST. BASIL THE GREAT (C. 330–79)

Blessing of the Kindling

I will kindle my fire this morning
In presence of the holy angels of heaven,
In presence of Ariel of the loveliest form,
In presence of Uriel of the myriad charms,
Without malice, without jealousy, without envy,
Without fear, without terror of anyone under the sun,
But the Holy Son of God to shield me.

> Without malice, without jealousy, without envy,
> Without fear, without terror of anyone under
>   the sun,
> But the Holy Son of God to shield me.

God, kindle Thou in my heart within
A flame of love to my neighbor,
To my foe, to my friend, to my kindred all,
To the brave, to the knave, to the thrall,
O Son of the loveliest Mary,
From the lowliest thing that liveth,
To the Name that is highest of all.
   O Son of the loveliest Mary,
   From the lowliest thing that liveth,
   To the Name that is highest of all.

—TRADITIONAL CELTIC BLESSING
(C. 500–C. 800)

The Creator's Power

You, all-accomplishing
Word of the Father,
are the light of primordial
daybreak over the spheres.
You, the foreknowing
mind of divinity,
foresaw all your works
as you willed them,
your prescience hidden
in the heart of your power,
your power like a wheel around the world,
whose circling never began
and never slides to an end.

—ST. HILDEGARD OF BINGEN (1098–1179)

Divine Love

Love
Gives herself to all things,
Most excellent in the depths,
And above the stars
Cherishing all:
For the High King
She has given
The kiss of peace.

— ST. HILDEGARD OF BINGEN (1098–1179)

Canticle of the Sun

Most High, all-powerful, good Lord,
Yours are the praises, the glory, the honor, and all blessing.
To You alone, Most High, do they belong,
and no man is worthy to mention Your name.
Praised be You, my Lord, with all your creatures,
especially Sir Brother Sun,
Who is the day and through whom You give us light.
And he is beautiful and radiant with great splendor;
and bears a likeness of You, Most High One.
Praised be You, my Lord, through Sister Moon and the
stars,
in heaven You formed them clear and precious and
beautiful.
Praised be You, my Lord, through Brother Wind,
and through the air, cloudy and serene, and every kind
of weather
through which You give sustenance to Your creatures.

Praised be You, my Lord, through Sister Water,
which is very useful and humble and precious and chaste.
Praised be You, my Lord, through Brother Fire,
through whom You light the night
and he is beautiful and playful and robust and strong.
Praised be You, my Lord, through our Sister Mother
   Earth,
who sustains and governs us,
and who produces varied fruits with colored flowers
   and herbs.
Praised be You, my Lord, through those who give
   pardon for Your love
and bear infirmity and tribulation.
Blessed are those who endure in peace
for by You, Most High, they shall be crowned.
Praised be You, my Lord, through our Sister Bodily
   Death,
from whom no living man can escape.
Woe to those who die in mortal sin.
Blessed are those whom death will find in Your most
   holy will,
for the second death shall do them no harm.
Praise and bless my Lord and give Him thanks
and serve Him with great humility.

— ST. FRANCIS OF ASSISI (C. 1181–1226)

The Beauty of Creation

Suppose a person entering a house were to feel heat on the
porch, and going farther, were to feel the heat increasing,
the more they penetrated within. Doubtless, such a person

would believe there was a fire in the house, even though they did not see the fire that must be causing all this heat. A similar thing will happen to anyone who considers this world in detail: one will observe that all things are arranged according to their degrees of beauty and excellence, and that the nearer they are to God, the more beautiful and better they are.

— ST. THOMAS AQUINAS (C. 1225–74)

The Divine Goodness

Because the divine goodness could not be adequately represented by one creature alone, God produced many and diverse creatures, that what was wanting in one in the representation of the divine goodness might be supplied by another. For goodness, which in God is simple and uniform, in creatures is manifold and divided. Thus the whole universe together participates in the divine goodness more perfectly and represents it better than any single creature whatever.

— ST. THOMAS AQUINAS (C. 1225–74)

Blessed Marie of the Incarnation

We, the chiefs and braves of the Huron nation, on our knees before Your Holiness present to you a precious perfume, the perfume of the virtues of Reverend Mother Mary of the Incarnation. . . . She it was who called us from the depths of our forests to teach us to know and

adore the true Master of life. Through her we learned to be meek. . . . Our mothers have kissed the imprint of her feet. With her hand she marked on our hearts the sign of the Faith and the Faith remained graven on our hearts. . . . Many a moon has passed since that first dawning of the true light upon us. Our nation, then great, is now threatened with complete extinction, but, Holy Father, we beg you to receive with the last wish and the last breath of the Huron Tribe the testimony of its profound gratitude to Reverend Mother Mary of the Incarnation.
(Blessed Marie of the Incarnation: 1599–1672)

— THE HURON

Pied Beauty

Glory be to God for dappled things—
    For skies of couple-color as a brinded cow;
      For rose-moles all in stipple upon trout that swim;
Fresh firecoal chestnut-falls; finches' wings;
    Landscapes plotted and pieced—fold, fallow, and
      plough;
      And all trades, their gear and tackle and trim.
All things counter, original, spare, strange;
    Whatever is fickle, freckled (who knows how?)
      With swift, slow; sweet, sour; adazzle, dim;
He fathers-forth whose beauty is past change:
      Praise him.

— GERARD MANLEY HOPKINS (1844 – 89)

Thistles for Some

How much you can learn, as I myself have learned, from watching cattle dreamily grazing and ruminating in their pastures! See how the sagacious creatures, without any theory or inflation of mind, instinctively select the herbs and grasses that suit and sustain them; and how they peacefully pass by what does not thus help them! They do not waste their time and energy in tossing away, or in trampling upon, or even simply in sniffing at, what is antipathetic to them. Why should they? Thistles may not suit them; well there are other creatures in the world whom thistles do suit. And, in any case, are they the police of this rich and varied universe?

— FRIEDRICH VON HÜGEL (1852–1925)

In No Strange Land

O world invisible, we view thee,
O world intangible, we touch thee,
O world unknowable, we know thee,
Inapprehensible, we clutch thee!

Does the fish soar to find the ocean,
The eagle plunge to find the air—
That we ask of the stars in motion
If they have rumor of thee there?

Not where the wheeling systems darken
And our benumb'd conceiving soars!—
The drift of pinions, would we hearken,
Beats at our own clay-shuttered doors.

The angels keep their ancient places;—
Turn but a stone, and start a wing!
'Tis ye, 'tis your estrangèd faces,
That miss the many-splendor'd thing.

But (when so sad thou canst not sadder)
Cry—and upon thy so sore loss
Shall shine the traffic of Jacob's ladder
Pitched between Heaven and Charing Cross.

Yea, in the night, my Soul, my daughter,
Cry—clinging heaven by the hems;
And lo, Christ walking on the water,
Not of Gennesareth, but Thames!

— FRANCIS THOMPSON (1859–1907)

Night Meditation

Night, most beautiful of the things I have made, it is you
that bring peace, you that bring rest to aching limbs, dislo-
cated by the day's work; you that calm, pacify, bring rest to
aching hearts, to bruised bodies—bodies bruised by work,
hearts bruised by labor and distress and daily cares. O my
black-eyed daughter, the only one who can be called my
accomplice. You aid and abet me, for you and I—I through
you—together we entrap man within my arms, taking him
as if by surprise. O night that binds up all wounds at the
well of the woman of Samaria, that from the profoundest
well draws the profoundest prayer. Night, O my daughter
Night, you know the art of silence, daughter of mine in
your beautiful cloak. You dispense rest and forgetfulness,
balm, silence, and shade. O starlit night, I created you

before all else, you that put to sleep, enshroud all my creatures in eternal darkness even now, you that put man to rest in the arms of my maternal Providence. Silence of the dark —such a silence reigned before the creation of unrest, before the start of the reign of unrest. A silence like this will reign—a silence though of light—when all this unrest shall have been expended, spent, when they shall have drawn all the water from the well, after the destruction, the consummation of all man's disquiet.

— CHARLES PÉGUY (1873–1914)

A Dazzling Darkness

Lord Jesus, when it was given me to see where the dazzling trail of particular beauties and partial harmonies was leading, I recognized that it was all coming to center on a single point, a single person: yourself. Every presence makes me feel that you are near me; every touch is the touch of your hand; every necessity transmits to me a pulsation of your will.

That the Spirit may always shine forth in me, that I may not succumb to the temptation that lies in wait for every act of boldness, nor ever forget that you alone must be sought in and through everything, you, Lord, will send me—at what moments only you know—deprivations, disappointments, sorrow.

What is to be brought about is more than a simple union: it is a transformation, in the course of which the only thing our human activity can do is, humbly, to make ourselves ready, and to accept.

— PIERRE TEILHARD DE CHARDIN (1881–1955)

Making Amends

The fundamental thing that has stayed with me has been the service of fellow men and women. As a young boy of five, I was given a very unusual opportunity of sharing for a time, the lives lived by shepherds, crofters, fishermen, grooms, fishwives, and hen wives. People who were illiterate, but were poets at heart. They filled my young life with ecstasy with their stories, songs, and dances. They were my tutors who opened a life to me that is unknown to most people. They prepared the way for me when I started off with my packsack full as I paddled across streams, climbed hills, gazed at the high mountains, and cherished the valleys, or caught something of the majesty and the mysteriousness of the oceans, the rivers, and the silence of the dense forests. . . .

The base of my commitment is thankfulness and reparation. A thankfulness for sensing beauty in so many different forms, for friendship, and for being in a position to help and to heal. Reparation to try in some way to make amends for the injustice and callousness that people of the western world caused to primitive peoples.

— TONY WALSH (1898 – 1994)

JESUS BORN

*A*fter their audience with the king they set out.
And behold, the star that they had seen at its
rising preceded them, until it came and stopped over
the place where the child was. They were overjoyed at
seeing the star, and on entering the house they saw the
child with Mary his mother. They prostrated themselves and did him homage. Then they opened their
treasures and offered him gifts of gold, frankincense,
and myrrh. And having been warned in a dream not
to return to Herod, they departed for their country by
another way.

—MATTHEW 2:9–12

Blessed Be

Blessed be the Child who today delights Bethlehem,
Blessed be the Newborn who today made humanity
   young again.
Blessed be the Fruit who bowed Himself down for our
   hunger.
Blessed be the Gracious One who suddenly enriched
   all of our poverty and filled our need.

Blessed be He whose mercy inclined Him to heal our
sickness. . . .

Blessed is He whom freedom crucified, when He
permitted it.

Blessed is He whom also the wood bore, when He
allowed it.

Blessed is He whom even the grave enclosed, when He
set limits to Himself.

Blessed is He whose will brought Him to the womb and
to birth and to the bosom and to growth.

Blessed is He whose changes revived our humanity.

Blessed is He who engraved our soul and adorned and
betrothed her to Him[self].

Blessed is He who made our body a Tabernacle for His
hiddenness.

Blessed is He who with our tongue interpreted His
secrets.

— ST. EPHRAEM THE SYRIAN (C. 306–73)

Strength Made Weak

The Maker of man was made man that the Ruler of the
stars might suck at the breast; that the Bread might be hun-
gered; the Fountain, thirst; the Light, sleep; the Way be
wearied with the journey; the Truth be accused by false
witnesses; the Judge of the living and the dead be judged
by a mortal judge; the Chastener be chastised with whips;
the Vine be crowned with thorns; the Foundation be hung
upon a tree; Strength be made weak; Health be wounded;
Life, die.

To suffer these and such like things, undeserved things, that he might free the undeserving, for neither did he deserve any evil, nor were we deserving of anything good, we who through him received such great good things; to suffer these, he who was before all ages, without any beginning of days, Son of God, deigned in these days to be the Son of man; and he who was begotten of the Father, not made by the Father, was "made" in the mother whom he had made; that here and now he might spring from her, who, except through him could no-when and no-where have been.

— ST. AUGUSTINE OF HIPPO (354 – 430)

This Marvelous Sharing

It is of no avail to say that our Lord, the son of the Virgin Mary, was true and perfect man, if he is not believed to be man of that stock from which the Gospel tells us he came.

Matthew says: "The book of the genealogy of Jesus Christ, the son of David, the son of Abraham." He then follows the order of Christ's human origin and traces the line of his ancestry down to Joseph, to whom the Lord's mother was betrothed.

Luke, on the other hand, works backward step by step and traces his succession to the first of the human race himself, to show that the first Adam and the last Adam were of the same nature.

The almighty Son of God could have come to teach and justify men with only the outward appearance of our humanity, exactly as he appeared to patriarchs and prophets. This he did when he wrestled with Jacob, or entered into

conversation, or when he did not refuse hospitable enter-
tainment, and even partook of the food set before him.

Those outward appearances pointed to this man.
They had a hidden meaning that proclaimed that his reality would be taken from the stock of his forefathers.

—— • ——

Hence God's plan for our reconciliation, formed before all
eternity, was not realized by any of these prefigurations. As
yet, the Holy Spirit had not come upon the Virgin nor had
the power of the Most High overshadowed her. Only then,
would the Word become flesh within her inviolate womb,
in which Wisdom would build a house for herself. Then,
too, the creator of ages would be born in time and the
nature of God would join with the nature of the slave in
the unity of one person. He through whom the world was
created would himself be brought forth in the midst of all
creation.

If the new man, made in the likeness of sinful flesh,
had not taken our old nature; if he, one in substance with
the Father, had not accepted to be one in substance with
the mother; if he who was alone free from sin had not
united our nature to himself—then men would still have
been held captive under the power of the devil. We would
have been incapable of profiting by the victor's triumph if
the battle had been fought outside our nature.

But, by means of this marvelous sharing, the mystery
of our rebirth shone out upon us. We would be reborn in
newness of spirit through the same Spirit through whom
Christ was conceived and born.

Consequently the evangelist speaks of those who believe as those "who were born, not of blood nor the will of the flesh nor of the will of man, but of God."

— ST. LEO THE GREAT (D. 461)

Under Your Wings

And you, Jesus, are you not also a mother?
Are you not the mother who, like a hen,
gathers her chickens under her wings?

Truly, Lord, you are a mother;
for both they who are in labor
and they who are brought forth
are accepted by you.

You have died more than they, that they may labor to
    bear.
It is by your death that they have been born,
for if you had not been in labor,
you could not have borne death;
and if you had not died, you would not have brought
    forth.
For, longing to bear sons into life,
you tasted of death,
and by dying you begot them.
You did this in your own self,
your servants by your commands and help.
You as the author, they as the ministers.
So you, Lord God, are the great mother.

— ST. ANSELM OF CANTERBURY (C. 1033–1109)

The Nativity of Christ

Behold the father is his daughter's son,
The bird that built the nest is hatched therein,
The old of years an hour hath not outrun,
Eternal life to live doth now begin,
The Word is dumb, the mirth of heaven doth weep,
Might feeble is, and force doth faintly creep.

O dying souls, behold your living spring;
O dazzled eyes, behold your sun of grace;
Dull ears, attend what word this Word doth bring;
Up, heavy hearts, with joy your joy embrace.
From death, from dark, from deafness, from despairs,
This life, this light, this Word, this joy repairs.

Gift better than himself God doth not know;
Gift better than his God no man can see.
This gift doth here the giver given bestow;
Gift to this gift let each receiver be.
God is my gift, himself he freely gave me;
God's gift am I, and none but God shall have me.

Man altered was by sin from man to beast;
Beast's food is hay, hay is all mortal flesh.
Now God is flesh and lies in manger pressed
As hay, the brutest sinner to refresh.
O happy field wherein this fodder grew,
Whose taste doth us from beasts to men renew.

— ST. ROBERT SOUTHWELL (1561–95)

To Stir Up the World

The prodigious expanses of time that preceded the first Christmas were not empty of Christ: they were imbued with the influx of his power. It was the ferment of his conception that stirred up the cosmic masses and directed the initial developments of the biosphere. It was the travail preceding his birth that accelerated the development of instinct and the birth of thought upon the earth. Let us have done with the stupidity that makes a stumbling block of the endless eras of expectancy imposed on us by the Messiah: the fearful, anonymous labors of primitive man, the beauty fashioned through its agelong history by ancient Egypt, the anxious expectancies of Israel, the patient distilling of the attar of oriental mysticism, the endless refining of wisdom by the Greeks: all these were needed before the Flower could blossom on the rod of Jesse and of all humanity. All these preparatory processes were cosmically and biologically necessary that Christ might set foot upon our human stage. And all this labor was set in motion by the active, creative awakening of his soul inasmuch as that human soul had been chosen to breathe life into the universe. When Christ first appeared . . . in the arms of Mary he had already stirred up the world.

— PIERRE TEILHARD DE CHARDIN (1881–1955)

One Body

It is truly a marvelous exchange: the creator . . . , taking a body, gives us his Godhead. The redeemer has come into the world to do this wonderful work. . . . One of us had broken the bond that made us God's children; one of us had to tie it again and pay the ransom. This could not be done by one who came from the old, wild, and diseased trunk; a new branch, healthy and noble, had to be grafted into it. He became one of us; more than this, he became one with us. For this is the marvelous thing about the human race, that we are all one. If it were otherwise, if we were all autonomous individuals, living beside each other quite free and independent, the fall of the one could not have resulted in the fall of all. In that case, on the other hand, the ransom might have been paid for and imputed to us, but his justice could not have been passed on to the sinners; no justification would have been possible. But he came to be one mysterious Body with us: he our head, we his members.

— ST. EDITH STEIN (1891–1942)

The Circle of a Girl's Arms

The circle of a girl's arms
have changed the world
the round and sorrowful world
to a cradle of God.

She has laid love in His cradle.
In every cot,
Mary has laid her child.

In each
comes Christ.
In each Christ comes
to birth,

comes Christ from the Mother's breast,
as the bird from the sun
returning,
returning again to the tree he knows
and the nest;
to last year's rifled nest.

Into our hands
Mary has given her child,
heir to the world's tears,
heir to the world's toil,
heir to the world's scars,
heir to the chill dawn
over the ruin of wars.

She has laid love in His cradle,
answering for us all.
"Be it done unto me."

— CARYLL HOUSELANDER (1901– 54)

Matthew's Magi

The Matthean infancy story is not only gospel (the good news of salvation)—it is the essential gospel story in miniature. And so, when we look back at the history of Christianity, perhaps we can understand better now why this infancy narrative has been one of the most popular sections of the whole Jesus story, one of the best known and of worldwide appeal. This was due not only to the appreciation of a good story that was satisfying to emotion and sentiment; it also reflected a Christian instinct recognizing therein the essence of the good news—that is, that

God has made himself present to us (Emmanuel) in the life of one who walked on this earth, indeed, so truly present that this one, Jesus, was his Son. This revelation was an offense and contradiction to some, but salvation to those who had eyes to see. Of the latter the magi are truly the forerunners, the anticipation of all those who would come to worship the risen Jesus proclaimed by the apostles.

— RAYMOND E. BROWN (1928 – 98)

JESUS
CRUCIFIED
AND RISEN

It was very early on the first day of the week and still dark, when Mary of Magdala came to the tomb. She saw that the stone had been moved away from the tomb and came running to Simon Peter and the other disciple, the one whom Jesus loved. "They have taken the Lord out of the tomb," she said, "and we don't know where they have put him."

So Peter set out with the other disciple to go to the tomb. They ran together, but the other disciple, running faster than Peter, reached the tomb first; he bent down and saw the linen cloths lying on the ground, but did not go in. Simon Peter, following him, also came up, went into the tomb, saw the linen cloths lying on the ground and also the cloth that had been over his head; this was not with the linen cloths but rolled up in a place by itself. Then the other disciple who had reached the tomb first also went in; he saw and he believed. Till this moment they had still not understood the scripture, that he must rise from the dead. The disciples then went back home.

—JOHN 20:I–IO

Descent into Hell

What is happening? Today there is a great silence over the earth, a great silence, and stillness, a great silence because the King sleeps; the earth was in terror and was still, because God slept in the flesh and raised up those who were sleeping from the ages. God has died in the flesh, and the underworld has trembled.

Truly he goes to seek out our first parent like a lost sheep; he wishes to visit those who sit in darkness and in the shadow of death. He goes to free the prisoner Adam and his fellow prisoner Eve from their pains, he who is God, and Adam's son.

The Lord goes in to them holding his victorious weapon, his cross. When Adam, the first created man, sees him, he strikes his breast in terror and calls out to all: "My Lord be with you all." And Christ in reply says to Adam: "And with your spirit." And grasping his hand he raises him up, saying: "Awake, O sleeper, and arise from the dead, and Christ shall give you light."

—— • ——

"I am your God, who for your sake became your son, who for you and your descendants now speak and command with authority those in prison: Come forth, and those in darkness: Have light, and those who sleep: Rise.

"I command you: Awake, sleeper, I have not made you to be held a prisoner in the underworld. Arise from the dead; I am the life of the dead. Arise, O man, work of my hands, arise, you who were fashioned in my image. Rise, let us go hence; for you in me and I in you, together we are one undivided person.

"For you, I your God became your son; for you, I the Master took on your form, that of slave; for you, I who am above the heavens came on earth and under the earth; for you, man, I became as a man without help, free among the dead; for you, who left a garden, I was handed over to Jews from a garden and crucified in a garden.

"Look at the spittle on my face, which I received because of you, in order to restore you to that first divine inbreathing at creation. See the blows on my cheeks, which I accepted in order to refashion your distorted form to my own image."

— • —

"See the scourging of my back, which I accepted in order to disperse the load of your sins, which was laid upon your back. See my hands nailed to the tree for a good purpose, for you, who stretched out your hand to the tree for an evil one.

"I slept on the cross and a sword pierced my side, for you, who slept in paradise and brought forth Eve from your side. My side healed the pain of your side; my sleep will release you from your sleep in Hades; my sword has checked the sword that was turned against you.

"But arise, let us go hence. The enemy brought you out of the land of paradise; I will reinstate you, no longer in paradise, but on the throne of heaven. I denied you the tree of life, which was a figure, but now I myself am united to you, I who am life. I posted the cherubim to guard you as they would slaves; now I make the cherubim worship you as they would God.

"The cherubim throne has been prepared, the bearers are ready and waiting, the bridal chamber is in order, the

food is provided, the everlasting houses and rooms are in
readiness, the treasures of good things have been opened;
the kingdom of heaven has been prepared before the ages."

— FROM "AN ANCIENT HOMILY
FOR HOLY SATURDAY"

The Lamb Slain

The prophets announced many wonderful things about
the Passover mystery that is Christ. To him be glory forever.
Amen.

He descended from heaven to earth for the sake of
suffering mankind, clothed himself with a human nature
through the Virgin Mary, and, appearing in our midst as a
man with a body capable of suffering, took upon himself
the suffering of those who suffered. By his Spirit, which
could not die, he slew death, the slayer of men. Led forth
like a lamb, slain like a sheep, he ransomed us from the
servitude of the world, just as he ransomed Israel from the
land of Egypt. He freed us from the slavery of the devil,
just as he had freed Israel from the hand of Pharaoh; and
he has marked our souls with the signs of his own blood.
He has clothed death with dishonor and he has grieved
the devil, just as Moses dishonored and grieved Pharaoh.
He has punished wickedness and taken away the children
of injustice, just as Moses punished Egypt and unchilded
it. He has brought us from slavery to freedom, from darkness to light, from death to life, from tyranny to an eternal
kingdom.

— • —

He is the Passover of our salvation. He was present in many so as to endure many things. In Abel he was slain; in Isaac bound; in Jacob a stranger; in Joseph sold; in Moses exposed; in David persecuted; in the prophets dishonored. He became incarnate of the Virgin. Not a bone of his was broken on the tree. He was buried in the earth, but he rose from the dead and was lifted up to the heights of heaven. He is the silent lamb, the slain lamb, who was born of Mary the fair ewe. He was seized from the flock and dragged away to slaughter. Toward evening he was sacrificed, and at night he was buried. But he who had no bone broken upon the cross, was not corrupted in the earth, for he rose from the dead and raised up man from the depths of the grave.

— ST. MELITO OF SARDIS (D. C. 190)

The New Vine

Since death could not devour him without a body and the world of the dead could not swallow him up without flesh, he came to the Virgin, so that he might receive from her a chariot on which to ride to the underworld. In the body he had assumed he entered death's domain, broke open its strong room, and scattered the treasure.

And so he came to Eve, the mother of all the living. She is the vineyard whose hedge death opened by Eve's own hands so that she might taste death's fruit. Thus Eve, the mother of all the living, became the source of death for all the living.

But Mary blossomed, the new vine compared with the old vine, Eve. Christ, the new life, lived in her, so that when death, brazen as ever, approached her in search of his prey, life, the bane of death, was hidden within her mortal fruit. And so when death, suspecting nothing, swallowed him up, death set life free, and with life a multitude of men. This glorious son of the carpenter, who set up his cross above the all-consuming world of the dead, led the human race into the abode of life. Because through the tree the human race had fallen into the regions below, he crossed over on the tree of the cross into the abode of life. The bitter shoot had been grafted onto the tree, and now the sweet shoot was grafted onto it so that we might recognize the one whom no creature can resist.

— ST. EPHRAEM THE SYRIAN (C. 306 – 73)

Exultet

Now let the angelic heavenly choirs exult; let joy pervade the unknown beings who surround God's throne; and let the trumpet of salvation sound the triumph of this mighty King. Let earth, too, be joyful, in the radiance of this great splendor. Enlightened by the glory of her eternal King, let her feel that from the whole round world the darkness has been lifted. Let mother Church likewise rejoice, arrayed in the brilliance of this dazzling light; let these walls echo with the multitude's full-throated song.

Dear brethren who are present at this wondrous lighting of the holy flame, I pray you join with me and invoke the loving-kindness of almighty God, that he who, not for any merit of mine, has deigned to number me among his ministers, may shed his own bright light upon me and enable me to glorify this candle with fitting praise, through our Lord Jesus Christ, his Son, who lives and reigns with him in the unity of the Holy Spirit, God; forever and ever.

It is indeed right and proper with all the ardor of our heart and mind and with the service of our voice to acclaim God, the invisible almighty Father, and his only-begotten Son, our Lord Jesus Christ, who repaid Adam's debt for us to his eternal Father, and with his dear blood erased the bond contracted through that ancient sin.

———— • ————

This is the Paschal feast wherein is slain the true Lamb whose blood hallows the doorposts of the faithful. This is the night when, long ago, thou didst cause our forefathers, the sons of Israel, in their passage out of Egypt, to pass dry-shod over the Red Sea. This is the night which swept away the blackness of sin by the light of the fiery pillar. This is the night which at this hour throughout the world restores to grace and yokes to holiness those who believe in Christ, detaching them from worldly vice and all the murk of sin. On this night Christ burst the bonds of death and rose victorious from the grave.

. . . What good would life have been to us without redemption? How wonderful the pity and care thou has shown us; how far beyond all reckoning thy loving-kindness! To ransom thy slave, thou gavest up thy Son! O truly necessary sin of Adam, that Christ's death blotted out; and happy fault, that merited so great a Redeemer! Blessed indeed is this, the sole night counted worthy to mark the season and the hour in which Christ rose again from the grave. It is this night of which the Scripture says: "And the night shall be bright as day." "Such is my joy that night itself is light!" So holy, this night, it banishes all crimes, washes guilt away, restores lost innocence, brings mourners joy; it drives forth hate, fosters harmony, and humbles the pride of earthly rule.

—— • ——

On this gracious night, then, holy Father, accept the evening sacrifice of this flame, which Holy Church, by the hands of her ministers, renders to thee in the solemn offering of wax the bees have made. Who now can doubt the message that this candle brings? A brilliant fire burns here to the glory of God, which though it be divided into parts, yet suffers no loss of light, being fed from the ever-melting wax that the parent bee brought forth to form the substance of this precious torch.

Blessed indeed is the night, which despoiled the Egyptians and enriched the Hebrews! The night on which heaven is wedded to earth, the Godhead to humanity!

We, therefore, pray thee, Lord, that this candle hallowed in honor of thy name, may continue bravely burning to dispel the darkness of this night. Welcome it as a sweet fragrance, mingling with the lights of heaven. May the morning-star find its flame alight, that Morning-Star which knows no setting, which came back from the grave and shed its clear light upon humankind.

— PASCHAL PROCLAMATION
(SEVENTH/EIGHTH CENTURY)

The Glory of the Cross

If there had been no cross, Christ would not have been crucified. If there had been no cross, Life would not have been nailed to the tree. If he had not been nailed, the streams of everlasting life would not have welled from his side, blood and water, the cleansing of the world; the record of our sins would not have been canceled, we would not have gained freedom, we would not have enjoyed the tree of life, paradise would not have been opened. If there had been no cross, death would not have been trodden underfoot, the underworld would not have yielded up its spoils.

How great the cross, through which we have received a multitude of blessings, because, against all reckoning, the miracles and sufferings of Christ have been victorious! How precious, the means of God's suffering, and his trophy of victory! On it of his own will he suffered unto death. On it he won his victory, wounding the devil, and conquering death, and shattering the bars of the underworld. The cross has become the common salvation of the whole world.

—— • ——

The cross is called the glory of Christ, and his exaltation; it is the chalice for which he longed, the consummation of his sufferings on our behalf. It is the glory of Christ—listen to his words: "Now is the Son of man glorified, and God is glorified in him, and God will glorify him at once." And again: "Glorify me, Father, with the glory that I had with you before the world was made." And again: "Father, glorify your name." So there came a voice from the heavens:

"I have glorified it, and I will glorify it again." By this he
means the glory that Christ received on the cross.

The cross is also Christ's exaltation—listen again to
his own words: "When I am lifted up, I will draw all men
to myself." You see then that the cross is the glory and the
exaltation of Christ.

— ST. ANDREW OF CRETE (C. 660 –740)

The Dream of the Rood

Hearken, the rarest of dreams I purpose to tell
Which I dreamed one midnight
When men with their voices were at rest.
It seemed to me that I saw a most wondrous tree
Rising in the sky and encircled with light,
Brightest of beams. The whole of the beacon
Was decked in gold. Gems gleamed
Fair at the earth's four corners, and five there were
High up on the cross-beam. Hosts of angels beheld it,
Timeless in their beauty. It was no felon's gibbet,
Rather, it held the gaze of holy souls,
Of men on the earth and the whole glorious creation.
Wondrous, this triumphant tree, and I stained with vice,
Sore wounded with sins. I gazed on the tree of glory,
Royally decked as it was, gleaming brightly,
Attired in gold: gems had covered
Befittingly the tree of a Ruler.
Yet beneath that gold I could make out agony
Once suffered at the hands of wretched men.
Soon it ran sweat on its right side. . . .

So lay I there for a long time,
Gazing sad at heart on a healer's tree
Till I heard it give voice,
Uttering words, this most precious wood:
"It was long since—yet I well remember—
That I was hewn down at wood-edge,
Struck off from my stem.
Men bore me on their shoulders, setting me on a hill
Where foes aplenty fastened me. Then I saw Man's Lord
Hasten with great courage, intent on climbing me.
Durst I not then oppose the word of the Lord
And bend or break, though I saw tremble
The surface of earth. All those foes
I could have felled, yet I stood firm.
Then the young warrior—it was God Almighty—
Stalwart, resolute, stripped himself; climbed the high
    gallows
Gallantly before the throng, resolved to loose Man's
    bonds.
Trembled I when this warrior embraced me
Yet durst I neither bow nor fall. I must needs stand fast.
As a rood I was raised up, bearing a noble king,
The heavens' lord; waver I durst not.
With dark nails they pierced me, leaving scars yet visible,
Open strokes of malice. Yet harm them I might not.
Each of us two they reviled at once. I stood drenched
    with blood
Poured forth from his side when he yielded up his
    spirit. . . .
All creation wept,
Lamenting a king's fall. It was Christ who hung there
    on a cross."

O Gentle Gatekeeper

O gentle gatekeeper!
O humble Lamb!
You are the gardener,
and once you have opened the gate of the heavenly
  garden,
paradise,
you offer us the flowers
and the fruits
of the eternal Godhead.
And now I know for certain
that you spoke the truth
when you appeared to your two disciples
on the road
as a traveler.
You said that Christ had to suffer so,
and by the way of the cross
enter into his glory.
And you showed them
that it had been foretold thus
by Moses,
Elijah,
Isaiah,
David,
and the others who had prophesied about you.
You explained the Scriptures to them,
but they failed to understand
because their minds were darkened.
But you understood yourself.
What then was your glory,
O gentle loving Word?

You yourself—
and you had to suffer
in order to enter into your very self!

— ST. CATHERINE OF SIENA (C. 1347–80)

Night

Every man has the right to bury his son. Every man on earth who has had the great misfortune not to have died before his son. I alone, I, God—my hands tied by this affair—I alone, father at the end of a long line of fathers, I alone could not bury my son. It was then, O Night, that you came and with an enormous shroud you enveloped the centurion with his Romans, the Virgin and the holy women, this mountain, that valley, over which the dark descended: over my people Israel, and over sinners and, with them all, the dying man, the man who was dying for them, and over the servants of Joseph of Arimathea, already approaching with a white shroud.

O Night, so dear to the heart for what you have done! What you did for my son made man in your great love, you do for all his brothers. You enwrap them in silence and shadow and in life-giving forgetfulness of the day's deadly unrest. What you did once for my son made man, what you did one evening above all evenings, you do again every evening for the least of men—so true is it, so real is it that he was become one of them, tied to their mortal condition without limit or measure. For before this perpetual, this imperfect, this perpetually imperfect imitation of Christ men speak of endlessly, there was Christ's perfect imitation of man, the relentless imitation by Christ Jesus of the mortal wretchedness and condition of man.

— CHARLES PÉGUY (1873–1914)

Veneration of the Cross

Many pass by the unveiled cross. Many remain. Because they belong there. Because here they have found everything. They stay. They kneel down. . . . Sinners kiss the wounds that they themselves have caused. The murderers flee from their guilt to the murdered One, the executioners to their own victim. And so I go to him. And sinners, who themselves are crucified with him on the cross of their own guilt, speak: "Lord, think of me when you come into your kingdom."

The dying lie at his feet. For they suffer his destiny. They die because he died. True, everyone must die because of sin. But God has allowed this deadly guilt in his kingdom of this world for a reason. He held this world embraced in his love for his incarnate Son, in whose death he was so able to overcome sin through greater grace that the world could not escape his mercy. And therefore death, which we ourselves caused and which we suffer as the wages of sin, is first, last, and always only the death that causes the death of sin.

Those who suffer weep before his cross. What night of need was not his night? What fears are not sanctified by his? To be raised up in hope, what grief needs to know more than that it has been borne by the Son of Man, who is the Son of God?

—•—

Before him the children kneel. For he has loved them, and although he knew what is in each person, he relied on them and threatened with his woe whoever scandalized one of these little ones.

Before him kneel the old people, who—let us be honest—have nothing more in sight and can count on nothing but to die. They kneel before their dying God. And they know that the greatest grace and hardest act of their lives are still to come. Only the man who dies in him and with him receives this grace rightly and carries out the act perfectly.

Before him kneel the homeless, and they gaze upon him who willed to die abandoned by his own people, outside the city near the highway, after living a hard life, not knowing where he would lay his head, poorer than the foxes, who have their dens.

The lonely kneel silently before him. For, as he was dying, the loneliest man of all, he knew them in the solitude of death and of abandonment by God. And he allowed all their bitter loneliness into his own heart, until everything else was driven out, except love for the abandoned.

——— • ———

Widows and mothers who have lost their sons kneel before him, weeping. For his eyes still look lovingly and with concern through the dark shadows of death that surround him, upon the mother whom he must leave lonely.

Lovers prostrate themselves before the crucified. For with him is all the strength of love and all the strength that turns the disillusion of love into that love that is stronger than death, into that unique love of Christ that can feed on its own fire and stay alive.

Before the cross the scholars and wise men of this world kneel. They learn thereby that all wisdom that does not burn in the blessed foolishness of love is vain; they learn thereby that the logic of the cross, which to the Greeks is folly and to the Jews a scandal, is God's wisdom and God's strength for those who are saved by it. And they learn that it has pleased God to save the world through the folly of the cross, before which every mouth is dumb and all the wisdom of the world humbles itself—before the folly of divine love.

God's priests kneel before the cross, because they have to preach the cross and they are always drinking from the chalice of his failure. They kneel there because, with their sins and weakness, they are always putting themselves between God's light and men, because more than all others they need his mercy.

— KARL RAHNER (1904 – 84)

ENCOUNTERING THE EXTRAORDINARY: THE SPIRIT, SAINTS, AND ANGELS

The Holy Spirit is an elusive and multifaceted entity. In Scripture, the Spirit is the creative, life-giving energy of God and a means by which humans can know and love God.

Angels can be understood as personifications of the Holy Spirit. They appear as messengers and agents of God. The saints are also agents of the Spirit. The Spirit makes possible their lives of exemplary holiness. The devotion that Christians render to Mary and the saints is an expression of the fundamental unity of Christians created by the persistent, dynamic, work of the Holy Spirit.

THE COMING
OF THE
SPIRIT

*W*hen *the time for Pentecost was fulfilled, they were all in one place together. And suddenly there came from the sky a noise like a strong driving wind, and it filled the entire house in which they were. Then there appeared to them tongues as of fire, which parted and came to rest on each one of them. And they were all filled with the holy Spirit and began to speak in different tongues, as the Spirit enabled them to proclaim.*

Now there were devout Jews from every nation under heaven staying in Jerusalem. At this sound, they gathered in a large crowd, but they were confused because each one heard them speaking in his own language. They were astounded, and in amazement they asked, "Are not all these people who are speaking Galileans? Then how does each of us hear them in his own native language? We are Parthians, Medes, and Elamites, inhabitants of Mesopotamia, Judea and Cappadocia, Pontus and Asia, Phrygia and Pamphylia, Egypt and the districts of Libya near Cyrene, as well as travelers from Rome, both Jews and converts to Judaism, Cretans and Arabs, yet we hear them speaking in our own tongues of the mighty acts of God." They were all astounded and bewildered, and

said to one another, "What does this mean?" But others
said, scoffing, "They have had too much new wine."

—ACTS 2:1–13

Invoking the Spirit

Father, you are holy indeed,
and all creation rightly gives you praise.
All life, all holiness comes from you
through your Son, Jesus Christ our Lord,
by the working of the Holy Spirit.

From age to age you gather a people to yourself,
so that from east to west
a perfect offering may be made
to the glory of your name.

And so, Father, we bring you these gifts.
We ask you to make them holy by the power of your
   Spirit,
that they may become the body and blood
of your Son, our Lord Jesus Christ,
at whose command we celebrate this eucharist.

— THIRD EUCHARISTIC PRAYER

Calming the Waters

Those who are engaged in spiritual warfare must always
keep their hearts tranquil. Only then can the mind sift the
impulses it receives and store in the treasure-house of the

memory those that are good and come from God, while rejecting altogether those that are perverse and devilish.

When the sea is calm, the fishermen's eyes can see the movements of the fish deep down, so that hardly any of them can escape. But when the sea is ruffled by the wind, the turmoil of the waves hides from sight the creatures that would easily have been seen if the sea wore the smile of calm. The skill of the fisherman is of little use in rough weather.

Something of the same sort happens with the soul, especially when it is stirred to the depths by anger.

At the beginning of a storm, oil is poured on the waters to calm them, and in fact the oil defeats their commotion. In this way, when the soul receives the anointing of the gift of the Holy Spirit, it gladly gives in to this inexpressible and untroubled sweetness. And even if it is continually attacked by temptation it maintains its peace and joy.

— DIADOCHUS OF PHOTICE (FIFTH CENTURY)

The Indwelling Spirit

A person is deemed worthy of constant prayer once he has become a dwelling place of the Spirit. For unless someone has received the gift of the Comforter, in all certainty he will not be able to accomplish this constant prayer in quiet.

But once the Spirit dwells in someone, as the Apostle says, the Spirit never ceases but prays continuously: then whether he sleeps or wakes, prayer is never absent from that person's soul. If he eats or drinks, goes to sleep or is active; yes, even if he is sunk in deep sleep, the sweet fragrance of prayer effortlessly breathes in his heart. Then he is in the possession of prayer that knows no limit. For at all times, even when he is outwardly still, prayer constantly ministers within him secretly.

The silence of the serene is prayer, as one of those clothed in Christ says, for their thoughts are divine stirrings. The stirring of a pure mind constitutes still utterances, by means of which such people sing in a hidden way to the hidden God.

— ISAAC OF NINEVEH (D. C. 700)

Come Down, O Love Divine

Come down, O love divine,
Seek thou this soul of mine,
And visit it with thine own ardor glowing;
O Comforter draw near,
Within my heart appear,
And kindle it, thy holy flame bestowing.

O let it freely burn,
Till earthly passions turn
To dust and ashes in its heat consuming;
And let thy glorious light
Shine ever on my sight,
And clothe me round, the while my path illuming.

Let holy charity
Mine outward vesture be,
And lowliness become mine inner clothing.
True lowliness of heart,
Which takes the humbler part,
And o'er its own shortcomings weeps with loathing.

And so the yearning strong,
With which the soul will long,
Shall far outpass the power of human telling;
For none can guess its grace,
Till he become the place
Wherein the Holy Spirit makes his dwelling.

—BIANCO DA SIENA (D. 1412)

Come, Holy Spirit

You do not remain, Holy Spirit, in the unmoved Father, nor in the Word, and yet you are always in the Father and in the Word and in yourself, and in all blessed spirits and creatures. All creatures need you, since the only-begotten Word, by shedding his blood, in his burning love placed all creatures in need of him. You repose in creatures who dispose themselves so that, by receiving your gifts, they may in purity receive your own image in themselves. You repose in those who receive in themselves the effect of the blood of the Word, and make themselves worthy dwelling places for you.

Come, Holy Spirit. May the union of the Father and the will of the Son come to us. You, Spirit of truth, are the reward of the saints, the refreshment of souls, light in darkness, the riches of the poor, the treasury of lovers, the satisfaction of the hungry, the consolation of the pilgrim Church; you are he in whom all treasures are contained.

Come, you who, descending into Mary, caused the Word to take flesh: effect in us by grace what you accomplished in her by grace and nature.

Come, you who are the nourishment of all chaste thoughts, the fountain of all clemency, the summit of all purity.

Come, and take away from us all that hinders us from being absorbed in you.

—ST. MARY MAGDALEN DEI PAZZI (1566–1607)

God's Grandeur

The world is charged with the grandeur of God.
    It will flame out, like shining from shook foil;
    It gathers to a greatness, like the ooze of oil
Crushed. Why do men then now not reck his rod?
Generations have trod, have trod, have trod;
    And all is seared with trade; bleared, smeared with
        toil;
    And wears man's smudge and shares man's smell:
        the soil
Is bare now, nor can foot feel, being shod.

And for all this, nature is never spent;
    There lives the dearest freshness deep down things;
And though the last lights off the black West went
    Oh, morning, at the brown brink eastward, springs—
Because the Holy Ghost over the bent
    World broods with warm breast and with ah! bright
        wings.

—GERARD MANLEY HOPKINS (1844 – 89)

The Satin Slipper

When the wind blows, the windmills go wheeling round all together.

But there is another Wind, I mean the Spirit, which is sweeping nations with a broom.

When you have it unchained, it sets all the human landscape a-moving.

Ideas from one end of the world to the other are catching fire like stubble!

From Thames to Tiber is heard a great clatter of arms and of hammers in the shipyards.

The sea is at one stroke all covered with white poppies, the night is plastered all over with Greek letters and algebraic signs.

There's dark America yonder like a whale bubbling out of the Ocean! Hark! Howling Asia feels a new god leaping in her womb!

And look at that fiery lover, what does he say? I think he has found the right word at last: look at that proud lady whose head droops and who crumbles piecemeal like a wall!

In all those things there is not any logical sequence, but please climb to the top of a tree with me, ladies and gentlemen.

Then you will understand all things, simply by seeing them together; they are all parts of one wide panorama.

All is contrived somehow by that fierce wind blowing without intermission, and the meaning of all.

To find it you need only to look up at that rude horseplay in the clouds, that disheveled cavalry in the singing sky with that untiring trumpet!

It could not last any longer! It is the same mouth everywhere clamoring for air; it is the same deep heart that says: Open here!

— PAUL CLAUDEL (1868–1955)

OUR LADY

My soul proclaims the greatness of the Lord;
    my spirit rejoices in God my savior.
For he has looked upon his handmaid's lowliness;
    behold, from now on will all ages call me
    blessed.
The Mighty One has done great things for me,
    and holy is his name.
His mercy is from age to age
    to those who fear him.
He has shown might with his arm,
    dispersed the arrogant of mind and heart.
He has thrown down the rulers from their thrones
    but lifted up the lowly.
The hungry he has filled with good things;
    the rich he has sent away empty.
He has helped Israel his servant,
    remembering his mercy,
according to his promise to our fathers,
    to Abraham and to his descendants forever.

—LUKE I:46–55

The Annunciation

In the sixth month, the angel Gabriel was sent from God to a town of Galilee called Nazareth, to a virgin betrothed to a man named Joseph, of the house of David, and the virgin's name was Mary. And coming to her, he said, "Hail, favored one! The Lord is with you." But she was greatly troubled at what was said and pondered what sort of greeting this might be. Then the angel said to her, "Do not be afraid, Mary, for you have found favor with God. Behold, you will conceive in your womb and bear a son, and you shall name him Jesus. He will be great and will be called Son of the Most High, and the Lord God will give him the throne of David his father, and he will rule over the house of Jacob forever, and of his kingdom there will be no end." But Mary said to the angel, "How can this be, since I have no relations with a man?" And the angel said to her in reply, "The holy Spirit will come upon you, and the power of the Most High will overshadow you. Therefore the child to be born will be called holy, the Son of God. And behold, Elizabeth, your relative, has also conceived a son in her old age, and this is the sixth month for her who was called barren; for nothing will be impossible for God." Mary said, "Behold, I am the handmaid of the Lord. May it be done to me according to your word." Then the angel departed from her.

— LUKE 1:26 – 38

Son of Mary

Scripture says that the Word of God was made flesh, that is, that he was united to flesh, which had a rational soul. The Word of God took to himself descent from Abraham and shared in flesh and blood, forming for himself a body from a woman, so that he should not only be God but should become man too and be regarded as one of our race because of his union with us.

Emmanuel therefore is made up of two realities, divinity and humanity, as we must acknowledge. But the Lord Jesus Christ is one, the one true Son, who is both God and man. He is not deified as we are by grace, but rather is true God made manifest in human form for us. St. Paul confirms this with his words: "When the fullness of time came, God sent forth his Son, born of a woman, born under the law; to redeem those who were under the law, so that we might receive adoption as sons."

— ST. CYRIL OF ALEXANDRIA (C. 375 – 444)

The Immaculate Conception

Lo, thou the glory of the great earth,
purest of women over all the world
of all who have been since time began
how right it is that all voices,
all heroes on earth, hail thee, and say
with blithe mood that thou art the bride
of the Noblest One, the sky's King.
So too the highest in the heavens,
Christ's thanes, cry out and sing

that thou art Lady by thy holy might
of the glorious armies, of the race of men
living under the heavens, and of all hell-dwellers.
For thou alone of all mankind
thought gloriously in thy strong mind
that thou wouldst bring to thy Maker thy maidenhood,
give it, sinless.

Not again
will such another come of men
a maiden ring-adorned who will thus send
heaven-homeward with ever pure heart
her bright treasure. So the Lord of triumphs
bade His high messenger fly hither
from his strong glory, and say to thee
that His might should speed thee, and thou shouldst bear
the Lord's Son, coming soon
in mercy to men, and thou, Maria,
forever and ever be held unstained.

— CYNEWULF (NINTH CENTURY)

The Sun Rides Forth

Sing the Dawn, holy Church,
The Immaculate Daybreak
In which Eternity, Creator, was himself created.
Sing the Dawn: Innocence, the skies are shaken
And the Sun rides forth, the Sun of all joys,
The Sun who made you, dazzling whiteness, empurpled
By redemptive flames which protected you
From the night which covered the heavens

When you were born, who now possess him within you.
The sun will leap and the world tremble
And the earth give birth
For you have given it fruitfulness,
Light whence falls the dew
Of the Mystery which enkindles you as you lean
   toward us
To bring him; smiling majesty and greatness of the Word
Which fills you, Flower full of sweetness.
Drawn by your fragrance the Bee flies down to you
From the splendor of the Father,
Your calyx closes round him
And shuts him in.

—ST. HILDEGARD OF BINGEN (1098–1179)

Mary Our Mother

Let us come to his bride, let us come to his mother, let us come to the best of his handmaidens. All of these descriptions fit Blessed Mary.

But what are we to do for her? What sort of gifts shall we offer her? O that we might at least repay to her the debt we owe her! We owe her honor, we owe her devotion, we owe her love, we owe her praise. We owe her honor because she is the Mother of our Lord. He who does not honor the mother, will without doubt dishonor the son. Besides, Scripture says: "Honor your father and your mother."

What then shall we say, brethren? Is she not our mother? Certainly, brethren, she is in truth our mother. Through her we are born, not to the world but to God.

We all, as you believe and know, were in death, in the infirmity of old age, in darkness, in misery. In death because we had lost the Lord; in the infirmity of old age, because we were in corruption; in darkness because we had lost the light of wisdom, and so we had altogether perished.

———•———

But through Blessed Mary we all underwent a much better birth than through Eve, inasmuch as Christ was born of Mary. Instead of the infirmity of age we have regained youth, instead of corruption incorruption, instead of darkness light.

She is our mother, mother of our life, of our incorruption, of our light. The Apostle says of our Lord, "Whom God made our wisdom, our righteousness, our sanctification and redemption."

She therefore who is the mother of Christ is the mother of our wisdom, mother of our righteousness, mother of our sanctification, mother of our redemption. Therefore she is more our mother than the mother of our flesh. Better therefore is our birth that we derive from Mary, for from her is our holiness, our wisdom, our righteousness, our sanctification, our redemption.

Scripture says, "Praise the Lord in his saints." If our Lord is to be praised in those saints through whom he performs mighty works and miracles, how much more should he be praised in her in whom he fashioned himself, he who is wonderful beyond all wonder.

— ST. AELRED OF RIEVAULX (C. 1110 – 67)

Maiden, yet a Mother

Maiden, yet a Mother,
Daughter of thy Son,
High beyond all other—
Lowlier is none;
Thou the consummation
Planned by God's decree,
When our lost creation
Nobler rose in thee!

Thus his place prepared,
He who all things made
'Mid his creatures tarried,
In thy bosom laid;
There his love he nourished,
Warmth that gave increase
To the Root whence flourished
Our eternal peace.

Nor alone thou hearest
When thy name we hail;
Often thou art nearest
When our voices fail;
Mirrored in thy fashion
All creation's good,
Mercy, might, compassion
Grace thy womanhood.

Lady, lest our vision
Striving heavenward, fail,
Still let thy petition
With thy Son prevail,
Unto whom all merit,

Power and majesty,
With the Holy Spirit
And the Father be.

— DANTE ALIGHIERI (1265 –1321)

The Perfect Mediator

God wills to love.
God wills to be loved.
God wills to have co-lovers of himself.

The perfect mediator
has to effect a perfect mediation
in respect of the person in whose favor he mediates
and in the perfection of his function as mediator.
Mary was the one above all
for whom he became mediator
therefore Christ achieved
the most perfect mediation and redemption
in his own function as mediator and redeemer
in regard to Mary.

— BLESSED JOHN DUNS SCOTUS (C. 1266 –1308)

The Redeemer

Christ was able to redeem others.
He has indeed redeemed us through the Cross
so as to attract us to his love
and because he willed
that men and women should be more worthy
of the love of God.

—BLESSED JOHN DUNS SCOTUS (C. 1266–1308)

Our Gracious Mother

Our natural mother, our gracious mother—for he willed wholly to become our mother in all things—humbly and gently found the place to begin his work in the maiden's womb. And he showed this in the first Showing, where he brought that gentle maid into my mind's eye, at the tender age she was when she first conceived. That is to say, it was in this humble place that our high God, who is the sovereign wisdom of all, set himself to grow, and clothed himself in our poor flesh so that he himself could undertake the work and care of motherhood in all things.

A mother's care is the closest, nearest, and surest—for it is the truest. This care never might, nor could, nor should, be fully done except by him alone. We know our own mother bore us into pain and dying. But our true Mother Jesus, who is all love, bears us into joy and endless living. Blessed may he be!

And so he nourished us within himself for love, and he labored until the full term, because he willed to suffer the sharpest pangs and deepest pains that ever were or ever shall be. And at the end he died. And when he had done this—and so borne us into bliss—yet even all this could not assuage his marvelous love. And he showed this in those high, wonderful words of love: "If I could have suffered more, I would have suffered more."

—JULIAN OF NORWICH (C. 1342 – C. 1420)

By Grace and Glory

God, the Incomprehensible, allowed himself to be perfectly comprehended and contained by the humble Virgin Mary without losing anything of his immensity. So we must let ourselves be perfectly contained and led by the humble Virgin without any reserve on our part.

God, the Inaccessible, drew near to us and united himself closely, perfectly, and even personally to our humanity through Mary without losing anything of his majesty. So it is also through Mary that we must draw near to God and unite ourselves to him perfectly, intimately, and without fear of being rejected.

Lastly, He Who Is deigned to come down to us who are not and turned our nothingness into God, or He Who Is. He did this perfectly by giving and submitting himself entirely to the young Virgin Mary, without ceasing to be in time He Who Is from all eternity. Likewise it is through Mary that we, who are nothing, may become like God by grace and glory. We accomplish this by giving ourselves to her so perfectly and so completely as to remain nothing, as far as self is concerned, and to be everything in her, without any fear of illusion.

—ST. LOUIS GRIGNION DE MONTFORT (1673–1716)

The Lady Spoke to Me

One day, when I had gone with the two girls to collect wood by the bank of the river Gave, I heard a sound. I turned toward the meadow and saw that the trees were not moving at all. I looked up and saw a grotto. And I saw a Lady wearing a white dress with a blue sash. On each foot she had a yellow rose; her rosary was the same color.

When I saw her, I rubbed my eyes, I thought I must be mistaken. I put my hands in my pocket, where I kept my rosary. I wanted to make the sign of the cross, but I could not lift my hand to my forehead; it fell back. Then the Lady crossed herself. I again tried, and although my hand was trembling, I was eventually able to make the sign of the cross. I began to say my rosary. The Lady slipped the beads of her rosary through her fingers, but she did not move her lips. When I finished the rosary, she immediately disappeared.

I asked the two girls if they had seen anything. They said, "No," and asked what I had to tell them. I told them that I had seen a Lady wearing a white dress but that I did not know who she was. But I warned them to keep silent about it. Then they urged me not to go back there, but I refused. I went back on Sunday, feeling drawn by an inner force.

—— • ——

The Lady spoke to me a third time and asked me if I was willing to come to her over a period of a fortnight. I replied that I was. She added that I must tell the priests to have a chapel built there. Then she told me to drink at the spring. Not seeing any spring, I was going to drink from the Gave. She told me that she did not mean that, and pointed with her finger to the spring. When I went there I saw only a little dirty water. I put my hand in it, but I could not get hold of any. I scratched, and at last a little water came for drinking. Three times I threw it away; the fourth time I was able to drink it. Then the vision disappeared, and I went away.

I went back there for fifteen days, and each day the Lady appeared to me, with the exception of a Monday and a Friday. She reminded me again to tell the priests to build the chapel, asked me to wash in the spring and to pray for the conversion of sinners. I asked her several times who she was, but she gently smiled at me. Finally, she held her arms outstretched and raised her eyes to heaven and told me that she was the Immaculate Conception.

During that fortnight she also revealed three secrets to me and forbade me to disclose them to anyone. I have kept them faithfully to this day.

— ST. BERNADETTE OF LOURDES (1844–79)

True Inner Peace

Many of us, who want to offer consolation, experience deep inner desolation. Many of us, who want to offer healing and affection to others, experience a seemingly inexhaustible hunger for intimacy. Many of us, who speak to others about the beauty of family life, friendship, and community, come home at night to a place that feels more like an empty cave than a true home. Many of us, who let water flow on the heads of those who search for a new family, give bread to those who search for a new community, and touch with oil those who search for healing, find ourselves with dry, hungry, and sick hearts, restless during the day and anxious during the night. Yes, indeed, many of us have lost touch with our identity as children of God.

But it is precisely this childhood that Mary wants us to claim. She, who offered an immaculate space for God to take on human flesh, wants to offer us also a space where we can be reborn as Jesus was born. With the same heart that she loved Jesus, she wants to love us. It is a heart that will not make us wonder anxiously whether we are truly loved. It is a heart that has not been marked by the infidelities of the human race and so will never bring wounds to those who seek peace there. Jesus has given her to us so that she could guide us in our search for a second childhood, assist us as we try to shake off our sadness, and open the way to true inner peace.

— HENRI J. M. NOUWEN (1932 – 96)

SAINTS AND ANGELS

*A*fter this I had a vision of a great multitude,
which no one could count, from every nation,
race, people, and tongue. They stood before the throne
and before the Lamb, wearing white robes and holding
palm branches in their hands. They cried out in a loud
voice:
   "Salvation comes from our God, who is seated on
      the throne,
         and from the Lamb."
All the angels stood around the throne and around
the elders and the four living creatures. They
prostrated themselves before the throne, worshiped
God, and exclaimed:
   "Amen. Blessing and glory, wisdom and
      thanksgiving,
         honor, power, and might
         be to our God forever and ever. Amen."

                                   —REVELATION 7:9–12

St. Martin of Tours Shares His Cloak

Martin happened to meet at the gate of the city of Amiens a poor man destitute of clothing. He was entreating those that passed to have compassion on him. . . .

Martin had nothing except the cloak in which he was clad, for he had already parted with the rest of his garments for similar purposes. Taking, therefore, his sword, with which he was girt, he divided his cloak into two equal parts and gave one part to the poor man, while he again clothed himself with the remainder. Upon this, some of the bystanders laughed, because he was now an unsightly object and stood out as but poorly dressed. Many, however, who were of sounder understanding, groaned deeply because they themselves had done nothing similar. . . .

In the following night when Martin had resigned himself to sleep, he had a vision of Christ arrayed in that part of his cloak with which he had clothed the poor man.

He contemplated the Lord with the greatest attention and was told to own as his own the robe that he had given. Ere long, he heard Jesus saying with a clear voice to the multitude of angels standing around—"Martin, who is still a catechumen, clothed me with this robe."
(St. Martin of Tours: c. 316–97)

At God's Beck and Call

So far as we are concerned, angels must be incorporeal or very near it. You see how we become dizzy with the theme and can get no further than the stage of being aware of angels and archangels, thrones, dominions, princedoms, powers, of glowing lights, ascents, intellectual powers or minds, beings of nature pure and unalloyed. Fixed, almost incapable of changing for the worse, they encircle God, the first cause, in their dance. What words can one use to hymn them? He makes them shine with purest brilliance or each with a different brilliance to match his nature's rank. So strongly do they bear the shape and imprint of God's beauty, that they become in their turn lights, able to give light to others by transmitting the stream that flows from the primal light of God.

As ministers of the divine will, powerful with inborn and acquired strength, they range over the universe. They are quickly at hand to all in any place, so eager are they to serve, so agile is their being. Each has under him a different part of the Earth or the universe, which God alone, who defined their ranks, knows. They unify the whole, making all things obey the beck and call of him alone who fashioned them. They hymn God's majesty in everlasting contemplation of everlasting glory, meaning, not to make God glorious—God, whose fullness supplies all else with excellence, cannot be added to—but to leave beings supreme after God with no kindness unshown them.

—ST. GREGORY OF NAZIANZUS (C. 329–90)

Preaching the Good News

I give thanks to my God tirelessly, who kept me faithful in the day of trial, so that today I offer sacrifice to him confidently, the living sacrifice of my life to Christ, my Lord, who preserved me in all my troubles. I can say therefore: Who am I, Lord, and what is my calling that you should cooperate with me with such divine power? Today, among heathen peoples, I praise and proclaim your name in all places, not only when things go well but also in times of stress. Whether I receive good or ill, I return thanks equally to God, who taught me always to trust him unreservedly. His answer to my prayer inspired me in these latter days to undertake this holy and wonderful work in spite of my ignorance, and to imitate in some way those who, as the Lord foretold, would preach his Good News as a witness to all nations before the end of the world.

How did I come by this wisdom that was not my own, I who neither knew what was in store for me, nor what it was to relish God? What was the source of the gift I got later, the great and beneficial gift of knowing and loving God, even if it meant leaving my homeland and my relatives?

—— • ——

I came to the Irish heathens to preach the Good News and to put up with insults from unbelievers. I heard my mission abused; I endured many persecutions even to the extent of chains; I gave up my freeborn status for the good of others. Should I be worthy, I am ready to give even my life, promptly and gladly, for his name; and it is there that I wish to spend it until I die, if the Lord should graciously allow me.

I am very much in debt to God, who gave me so much grace that through me many people were born again in God and afterward confirmed, and that clergy were ordained for them everywhere. All this was for a people newly come to belief whom the Lord took from the very ends of the earth as he promised long ago, through his prophets: "To you the nations will come from the ends of the earth and will say, 'How false are the idols our fathers made for themselves, how useless they are.'" And again: "I have made you a light for the nations so that you may be a means of salvation to the ends of the earth."

I wish to wait there for the promise of one who never breaks his word, as he promises in the Gospel: "They will come from the east and the west to take their places with Abraham and Isaac and Jacob," just as we believe the faithful will come from every part of the world.

— ST. PATRICK (C. 390 – C. 461)

Light of Light

In their goodness [the angels] raise their inferiors to become, so far as possible, their rivals. They ungrudgingly impart to them the glorious ray that has visited them so that their inferiors may pass this on to those yet farther below them. Hence, on each level, predecessor hands on to successor whatever of the divine light he has received and this, in providential proportion, is spread out to every being.

Of course God himself is really the source of illumination for those who are illuminated, for he is truly and really Light itself. He is the Cause of being and of seeing. But, in imitation of God, it has been established that each being is somehow superior to the one to whom he passes on the divine light. And so all the other angelic beings follow the first rank of intelligent beings in heaven as the source, after God, of all sacred knowledge of God and of all imitation of God, for it is this latter order that mediates the divine enlightenment to all other beings, including ourselves. . . .

Angels of the first rank possess, more than the others, the power of fire and a share of the divine wisdom that has been poured out to them, a knowledge of the ultimate in divine enlightenment, and that capacity that is summed up in the word *thrones.*

— PSEUDO-DIONYSIUS THE AREOPAGITE
(FIFTH/SIXTH CENTURY)

St. Columba

In the forty-second year of his age Colum Cille sailed away from Ireland to Britain, wishing to be a pilgrim for Christ. During his life of thirty-four years as a soldier of Christ on the island of Iona, he could not let even one hour pass that was not given to prayer or reading or writing or some other good work. Night and day he so unwearyingly gave himself to fasts and vigils that the burden of each single work seemed beyond the strength of man. Yet through all he was loving to everyone, his holy face was always cheerful, and in his inmost heart he was happy with the joy of the Holy Spirit.

When the end of his years was at hand, he gave his last commands to his brothers, saying: "I commend to you, my children, these last words of mine, that you keep among you unfeigned love with peace." Then when the bell was rung for the midnight office he arose quickly and went to the church, where he went in alone before the others and knelt down in prayer before the altar. Diormuit his attendant followed, and the whole community of monks ran in

with lights; when they saw that their father was dying they began to lament. Then Diormuit raised the saint's holy right hand, to bless the monastic company. At the same time the venerable father himself moved his hand, as well as he was able, and immediately after he had so expressed his holy blessing he breathed his last.
(St. Columba: 521–97)

— ST. ADAMNAN OF IONA (C. 625 –704)

Angels and Archangels

It must be realized that the word *angel* is the name of an office, and not of a nature. For these holy spirits of our homeland in heaven are always spirits, but in no way can they always be called "angels" or "messengers" since they are angels only when something is announced through them. Those who make minor announcements are called angels; those who make important ones are called archangels.

Hence it is that not just any angel was sent to the Virgin Mary but that Gabriel the archangel was sent: it was right that the proper one for this role should be of the highest rank of angels since he was to announce the greatest news of all.

Angels are known by proper names as well, to indicate their powers and their work. In that holy city where perfect knowledge is derived from the vision of Almighty God, if proper names are assigned to them, it is not that their persons could not be identified without names. But when angels come to minister to us, even the names by which we know them are taken from their ministry—

Michael means "Who is like God," Gabriel "Strength of God," Raphael "Healing of God."

———— • ————

Whenever a mighty deed is in question, Michael is assigned, so that by his actions and name it may be made known that no one can do what God can do. So in the case of our ancient enemy, who in his pride wanted to be like God when he said: "I will ascend to heaven; above the stars of God I will set my throne on high; I will make myself like the Most High": when he is shown to be condemned to eternal punishment at the end of the world, he is described as about to do battle with Michael, as St. John says: "War broke out with Michael the archangel."

Gabriel was sent to Mary, for Gabriel means "Strength of God." He came to announce him who deigned to be lowly so as to wage war on the spiritual powers of the air. He who came as God of power and as one strong in battle was to be announced by Gabriel, the strength of God.

Finally Raphael is interpreted, as we have said, as "Healing of God," since he wiped away the shadows of blindness from Tobias when he touched his eyes to cure him. The one who is sent to cure was indeed worthy of the name "Healing of God."

— ST. GREGORY THE GREAT (C. 540 – 604)

The Angelic Host

In God's love the angels live in concord and happiness. Each of them loves all the others, and all of them love each;

they all want the same things and all of them are averse to the same things; what pleases one is displeasing to none, and what one wants, they all want. There is one purpose and one will for all; all feel the same thing, and all sense the same thing. . . .

There is nothing disordered, nothing undisciplined, nothing contrary to order or obedience, nothing secretly put away with the intention of keeping it for oneself. Everything is open and aboveboard, everything is plain, and things that are proper to each individual are common to all through the sharing of love and the love of sharing. They are all assembled in one temple and raise their shouts of joy to God in common; all at the same time read and meditate and contemplate in the book of life; and they all refresh themselves communally at one and the same table. They take their rest together in the place of eternal repose, and there is no one who does anything on his own that can disturb or damage their common peace, obedience, or order.

Such is the fellowship—the happiest and most joyous of fellowships—of the citizens of the realms above who live the common life, and we who are still on earth should follow their way of life by living the common life after their example.

— BALDWIN OF CANTERBURY (D. 1190)

St. Dominic de Guzman, Herald of the Gospel

So noble in character, so ardently on fire with divine love was Dominic that there can be no doubt that he was a chosen vessel of grace. Except when he was moved to pity and compassion he always displayed great firmness of mind. A joyous heart is reflected in the countenance, and Dominic revealed his tranquillity of soul by the joyful kindliness of his look.

Everywhere, in word and in deed, he showed himself to be a herald of the gospel. By day no one was more affable, more friendly than he with his brethren and companions, no one more fervent than he in vigils and prayer at night. His conversation was always either with God or about God; rarely did he speak on other matters, and this practice he commended to his disciples.

Dominic's frequent and special prayer for himself was to beg from God true and efficacious charity for the salvation of men, for he was convinced that just as our Savior, the Lord Jesus, gave himself totally for our salvation, only when he, Dominic, had devoted himself to the winning of souls would he be truly a member of Christ. When he had pondered the matter long and deeply he founded the Order of Preachers for this very purpose.

— • —

Dominic often exhorted the friars, both in his writings and by his words, to study constantly the sacred scriptures, in the old and new testaments. He always carried a copy of the gospel according to St. Matthew and the epistles of

St. Paul; these he had studied to such an extent that he almost knew them off by heart.

Several times Dominic was chosen as bishop, but he always refused the office, preferring to live in poverty with his brethren, than to possess any bishopric. All his life long he preserved his purity intact. He longed ardently to be beaten, to be cut in little pieces, to die for his faith. Gregory IX declared: "I knew him as a wholehearted follower of the apostolic way of life, and there is no doubt that he shares in heaven the glory of the apostles themselves." *(St. Dominic de Guzman: c. 1170–1221)*

Guardian Angels

There is no creature, no matter how mean, vile, or abject, faithful or unfaithful, who has not his angel to guard him and to urge him continually to do right.

These blessed spirits offer our prayers to the divine Goodness; they kindle in our hearts the love of virtue; they strengthen us and obtain for us the courage and vigor to practice it—if we are sad and in adversity, they are ever near, to cheer us and exhort us to patience. They never cease to inspire us with good thoughts, to help us to make progress in divine love; until at last we reach the heavenly country, to dwell forever in their company.

This is what they desire, knowing that for this end we were created. They are so jealous of our happiness that they rejoice when they see that we are faithful to God and that we are corresponding with his love; and when we do not, if they could grieve they would. It is to our guardian angels that we owe all our good inspirations, suitable to our vocation and circumstances.

— ST. FRANCIS DE SALES (1567–1622)

St. Martin de Porres

St. Martin, in his total openness to Christ's teachings, loved his brethren with a love that sprang from humility and an unclouded faith. He loved men because he saw them as God's children and his own brothers. He loved them indeed more than himself, and in his humility believed everyone to be better and holier than he was.

He never failed to find excuses for the faults of others; he ignored even bitter slights and insults done to himself since he was quite convinced that his sins deserved far greater punishments. He made every effort to bring sinners to repentance: he nursed the sick devotedly, procuring food, clothes, and medicine for those too poor to buy them. Peons, negroes, and half-castes, who were treated as all but slaves, these he worked for to the limits of his abilities, offering them every help and tenderness until he truly deserved his popular title, "Martin the Charitable."
(St. Martin de Porres: 1579–1639)

— POPE JOHN XXIII (1881–1963)
IN A 1962 HOMILY

Maximilian Kolbe, Saint of Auschwitz

One of the prisoners on the parade ground at Auschwitz cried, "My poor wife and children!" It sounded strange and hopeless. Suddenly a slight figure stepped out of line, took off his cap, and moved with halting gait to stand at attention before the SS.

"What does this Polish pig want? Who are you?"

"I am a Catholic priest; I want to die for that man. I am old; he has a wife and children."

The deputy commandant signaled to the man with the family to return to his place in the line, and the numbers on the list were changed.

While the sun set in beauty over Auschwitz the condemned men were driven into the bunker, naked, humiliated, and afraid. But they were shepherded by a priest who went with them to die and to help them to die. Father Kolbe took charge of his suffering flock and filled their last days with prayer and psalms.

There were only four alive after two weeks and of these men only Kolbe was fully conscious. The authorities became impatient and ordered the head of the hospital barracks to inject phenol into the priest's veins. Father Kolbe was alone at the moment of his death: 12:50 P.M. on August 14, 1941, the Vigil of the Assumption. He was forty-seven years old.

(St. Maximilian Kolbe: 1894–1941)

— DIANA DEWAR

EXPERIENCING THE SACRED: SACRAMENTS AND PRAYER

The sacraments and prayer are our means to experience unity with God and each other. The Catholic Church has defined seven sacraments—Baptism, Eucharist, Confirmation, Reconciliation and Penance, Marriage, Holy Orders, and the Anointing of the Sick. But the notion of sacrament is broader than this. A sacrament is any manifestation of God's love and power in space and time. Jesus himself is the first sacrament and the mystery that lies at the heart of our relationship with God.

Prayer is our response to this great mystery. Says St. Thérèse of Lisieux, "For me, prayer is an uplifting of the heart, a glance toward heaven, a cry of gratitude and love in times of sorrow as well as joy. It is something, . . . which expands the soul and unites it to God."

CHURCH AND
SACRAMENTS

*H*e is the image of the invisible God,
 the firstborn of all creation.
For in him were created all things in heaven and on
 earth,
 the visible and the invisible,
 whether thrones or dominions or principalities or
 powers;
 all things were created through him and for him.
He is before all things,
 and in him all things hold together.
He is the head of the body, the church.
He is the beginning, the firstborn from the dead,
 that in all things he himself might be
 preeminent.
For in him all the fullness was pleased to dwell,
 and through him to reconcile all things for him,
 making peace by the blood of his cross
 [through him], whether those on earth or those in
 heaven.

—COLOSSIANS 1:15–20

Instructions to the
Newly Baptized at Jerusalem

You were conducted by the hand to the holy pool of sacred baptism, just as Christ was conveyed from the cross to the sepulchre close at hand.

Each person was asked if he believed in the name of the Father and of the Son and of the Holy Spirit. You made the confession that brings salvation, and submerged yourselves three times in the water and emerged: by this symbolic action you were secretly reenacting the burial of Christ three days in the tomb.

Just as our Savior spent three days and nights in the womb of the earth, so you upon first emerging were representing Christ's first day in the earth, and by your immersion his first night. For at night one can no longer see but during the day one has light; so you saw nothing when immersed as if it were night, but you emerged as if to the light of day. In one and the same action you died and were born: that water of salvation became both tomb and mother for you.

What Solomon said in another context is apposite to you: "There is a time to be born, and a time to die," but the opposite is true in your case—there is a time to die and a time to be born. A single moment achieves both ends, and your begetting was simultaneous with your death.

—— • ——

What a strange and astonishing situation! We did not really die, we were not really buried, we did not really hang from a cross and rise again. Our imitation was symbolic, but our salvation a reality.

Christ truly hung from a cross, was truly buried, and truly rose again. All this he did gratuitously for us, so that we might share his sufferings by imitating them, and gain salvation in actuality.

What boundless love! The innocent hands and feet of Christ were pierced by the nails: he suffered the pain. I suffer neither pain nor anguish: yet by letting me participate in his pain he gives me the free gift of salvation.

No one should think, then, that his baptism is merely for the remission of sins and for adoption as sons in the way that John's baptism brought only remission of sins. We know well that not merely does it cleanse sins and bestow on us the gift of the Holy Spirit—it is also the counterpart of Christ's suffering. This is why, as we heard just now, Paul cried out: "Do you not know that all of us who have been baptized into Christ Jesus were baptized into his death? We were buried therefore with him by baptism into death."

Christians in the World

The difference between Christians and the rest of mankind is not a matter of nationality, language, or customs. Christians do not live apart in separate cities of their own, speak any special dialect, nor practice any eccentric way of life. The doctrine they profess is not the invention of busy human minds and brains, nor are they, like some, adherents of this or that school of human thought.

They pass their lives in whatever township—Greek or foreign—each man's lot has determined; and conform to ordinary local usage in their clothing, diet, and other habits. Nevertheless, the organization of their community does exhibit some features that are remarkable, and even surprising. For instance, though they are residents at home in their own countries, their behavior there is more like that of transients; they take their full part as citizens, but they also submit to anything and everything as if they were aliens. For them, any foreign country is a motherland, and any motherland is a foreign country. Like other men, they marry and beget children, though they do not expose their infants. Any Christian is free to share his neighbor's table, but never his marriage bed.

—— • ——

Though destiny has placed them here in the flesh, they do not live after the flesh; their days are passed on the earth, but their citizenship is above in the heavens. They obey the prescribed laws, but in their own private lives they transcend the laws. They show love to all men—and all men persecute them. They are misunderstood and condemned; yet by suffering death they are quickened into life. They are poor, yet making many rich; lacking all things, yet having all things in abundance. They are dishonored, yet made glorious in their very dishonor; slandered, yet vindicated. They repay calumny with blessings, and abuse with courtesy. For the good they do, they suffer stripes as evildoers; and under the strokes they rejoice like men given new life. Jews assail them as heretics, and Greeks harass them with persecutions; and yet of all their ill-wishers there is not one who can produce good grounds for his hostility.

—— • ——

To put it briefly, the relation of Christians to the world is that of a soul to the body. As the soul is diffused through every part of the body, so are Christians through all the cities of the world. The soul, too, inhabits the body, while at the same time forming no part of it; and Christians inhabit the world, but they are not part of the world. The soul, invisible herself, is immured within a visible body; so Christians can be recognized in the world, but their Christianity itself remains hidden from the eye. The flesh hates the soul, and wars against her without any provocation, because she is an obstacle to its own self-indulgence; and the world similarly hates the Christians without provocation, because they are opposed to its pleasures.

All the same, the soul loves the flesh and all its members, despite their hatred for her; and Christians, too, love those who hate them. The soul, shut up inside the body, nevertheless holds the body together; and though they are confined within the world as in a dungeon, it is Christians who hold the world together. The soul, which is immortal, must dwell in a mortal tabernacle; the Christians, as they sojourn for a while in the midst of corruptibility here, look for incorruptibility in the heavens. Finally, just as to be stinted of food and drink makes for the soul's improvement, so when Christians are every day subjected to ill-treatment, they increase the more in numbers. Such is the high post of duty in which God has placed them, and it is their moral duty not to shrink from it.

—LETTER TO DIOGNETUS (C. SECOND CENTURY)

The Ship of the Church

The Church is like a great ship sailing the sea of the world and tossed by the waves of temptation in this life. But it is not to be abandoned—it must be brought under control.

As an example of this we have the Fathers of the past, Clement and Cornelius and many others in the city of Rome, Cyprian in Carthage and Athanasius in Alexandria. Living under pagan emperors, they steered the ship of Christ, that is the Church, his beloved spouse. And they did this by teaching, defending, working, and suffering even to the shedding of their blood.

When I considered the example of these men and of men like them, I was filled with fear. Dread came upon me and trembling, and the darkness of my sins almost overwhelmed me. I should have been only too glad to give up the government of the Church that I had accepted, if only I could have found some support for this course of action in the example of the Fathers or in sacred scripture.

— ST. BONIFACE (C. 675–754)

The Eucharistic Banquet

The only-begotten Son of God, wishing to enable us to share in his divinity, assumed our nature, so that by becoming man he might make men gods.

Moreover, he turned the whole of our nature, which he assumed, to our salvation. For he offered his body to God the Father on the altar of the cross as a sacrifice for our reconciliation; and he shed his blood for our ransom

and our cleansing, so that we might be redeemed from
wretched captivity and cleansed from all sins.

Now in order that we might always keep the mem-
ory of this great act of love, he left his body as food and his
blood as drink, to be received by the faithful under the appearances of bread and wine.

How precious and wonderful is this banquet, which
brings us salvation and is full of all delight! What could be
more precious? It is not the meat of calves or kids that is offered, as happened under the Old Law; at this meal Christ,
the true God, is set before us for us to eat. What could be
more wonderful than this sacrament?

No sacrament contributes more to our salvation than
this; for it purges away our sins, increases our virtues, and
nourishes our minds with an abundance of all the spiritual
gifts.

— ST. THOMAS AQUINAS (C. 1225 –74)

The Divine Mysteries

Suppose that this most holy Sacrament were celebrated in
one place only; suppose there were only one priest in the
whole world to say the words of consecration. How men
would long to go to that place, to visit that one priest of
God and see the divine mysteries celebrated! But now
there are many priests, and in many places Christ is offered, so that the farther afield Holy Communion is spread
throughout the world, the greater proof it may yield of
God's grace and love for men. Thank you, O good Jesus,
eternal shepherd, for deigning to refresh us poor outcasts
with your precious body and blood; for inviting us with

your own lips to partake of this mystery, when you say: Come to me, all you that labor and are burdened; I will give you rest. . . .

O Jesus, sweetest, kindest, what great worship and thanksgiving we ought to show you, what never-ending praise, in return for the gift of your holy body! There is not a man to be found able to unfold in words its wonderful power.

— THOMAS À KEMPIS (C. 1380–1471)

On the Eucharist

I have not yet said anything about the most sacred of all devotions—the holy and sacred sacrifice and sacrament of the Eucharist, the heart of the Christian religion. It is an ineffable mystery that embraces the untold depths of divine love, and in which God, giving himself to us, bestows freely upon us all his blessings and graces.

Prayer united to this divine sacrifice has unutterable power. Endeavor if possible to be present each day at holy Mass, so that together with the priest you may offer the sacrifice of your Redeemer to God his Father on your own behalf and that of the whole Church. What a privilege it is to be united in so blessed and mighty an action!

If you are unavoidably prevented from being present at the celebration of this great sacrifice by real and bodily presence, do not fail to join in it by a spiritual communion. So that, if you cannot go to church, at least go there in spirit, unite your intention with all your brethren, and offer the same spiritual service that you would offer if you were able to be present in person.

If you wish to make your daily meditation at this time, turn your mind to offering this sacrifice through your prayer and meditation.

— ST. FRANCIS DE SALES (1567–1622)

The Author of Life

Love of the "Blackrobes" is general among the Indians everywhere, even among the Sioux, a most savage tribe. A priest who has been among them and who often comes here tells me that they would supply all his needs were he willing to accept it, but that he does not want to be indebted to them for fear they ask him for firewater, that is, brandy. One Indian was strikingly converted. As he lay on his deathbed he spoke of a previous illness during which he had thought he was dying, and he said aloud: "I then saw the Author of Life and He said to me, 'Go back, your hour is not yet!' But I know that this time I shall go to the Author of Life." Francis, a Christian Iroquois present, said to him: "The Author of Life probably sent you back so that you might have water poured on your head." The dying Sioux made answer: "Indeed, I think it was precisely for that I was told to return to life." Francis replied: "Do you want me to go and get a Blackrobe to pour water upon you?" The Sioux answered: "Go quickly. There is need of haste." The priest who came at once was quite satisfied with the dying man's answers and baptized him; a few moments later he died. He was solemnly buried by the priest, who also baptized the dead Sioux's son who was very ill.

The priest was Father Acquaroni, a Lazarist from Rome, and one of our most zealous friends.

— ST. ROSE PHILIPPINE DUCHESNE (1769–1852)

Mass on the World

Since once again, Lord—though this time not in the forests of the Aisne but in the steppes of Asia—I have neither bread, nor wine, nor altar, I will raise myself beyond these symbols, up to the pure majesty of the real itself; I, your priest, will make the whole earth my altar and on it will offer you all the labors and sufferings of the world.

Over there, on the horizon, the sun has just touched with light the outermost fringe of the eastern sky. Once again, beneath this moving sheet of fire, the living surface of the earth wakes and trembles, and once again begins its fearful travail. I will place on my paten, O God, the harvest to be won by this renewal of labor. Into my chalice I shall pour all the sap that is to be pressed out this day from the earth's fruits.

My paten and my chalice are the depths of a soul laid widely open to all the forces that in a moment will rise up from every corner of the earth and converge upon the Spirit. Grant me the remembrance and the mystic presence of all those whom the light is now awakening to the new day.

— PIERRE TEILHARD DE CHARDIN
(1881–1955)

To Preach Christ Jesus

"Woe to me if I do not preach the gospel!" I am sent by Christ himself to do this. I am an apostle, I am a witness. The more distant the goal, the more difficult my mission, the more pressing is the love that urges me to it. I must bear witness to his name: Jesus is the Christ, the Son of the living God. He reveals the invisible God, he is the firstborn of all creation, the foundation of everything created. He is the teacher of mankind, and its redeemer. He was born, he died, and he rose again for us.

He is the center of history and of the world; he is the one who knows us and who loves us; he is the companion and friend of our life. He is the man of sorrows and of hope. It is he who will come and who one day will be our judge and—we hope—the everlasting fullness of our existence, our happiness.

I could never finish speaking about him: he is the light and the truth; indeed, he is the way, the truth, and the life. He is the bread and the spring of living water to satisfy our hunger and our thirst. He is our shepherd, our guide, our model, our comfort, our brother.

—— • ——

Like us, and more than us, he has been made little, poor, humiliated; he has been a worker; he has known misfortune and been patient. For our sake he spoke, worked miracles, and founded a new kingdom where the poor are happy, where peace is the principle for living together, where the pure of heart and those who mourn are raised up and comforted, where those who hunger and thirst after justice have their fill, where sinners can be forgiven, where all are brothers.

Jesus Christ: you have heard him spoken of; indeed the greater part of you are already his: you are Christians. So, to you Christians I repeat his name, to everyone I proclaim him: Jesus Christ is the beginning and the end, the Alpha and the Omega; he is the king of the new world; he is the secret of history; he is the key to our destiny. He is the mediator, the bridge, between heaven and earth. He is more perfectly than anyone else the Son of Man, because he is the Son of God, eternal and infinite. He is the son of Mary, blessed among all women, his mother according to the flesh, and our mother through the sharing in the Spirit of his mystical body.

Jesus Christ is our constant preaching; it is his name that we proclaim to the ends of the earth and throughout all ages.

— POPE PAUL VI (1897–1978)

PATHWAYS IN PRAYER

*I*n *praying, do not babble like the pagans, who think that they will be heard because of their many words. Do not be like them. Your Father knows what you need before you ask him. This is how you are to pray:*

> *Our Father in heaven,*
> > *hallowed be your name,*
> > *your kingdom come,*
> *your will be done,*
> > *on earth as in heaven.*
> *Give us today our daily bread;*
> > *and forgive us our debts,*
> > *as we forgive our debtors;*
> *and do not subject us to the final test,*
> > *but deliver us from the evil one.*

If you forgive others their transgressions, your heavenly Father will forgive you. But if you do not forgive others, neither will your Father forgive your transgressions.

*—*MATTHEW 6:7–15

Inexhaustible Fountain

The word of God is a tree of life that from all its parts of-
fers you fruits that are blessed. It is like that rock opened in
the desert that from all its parts gave forth a spiritual drink.
As the Apostle says, "All ate the same supernatural food and
all drank the same supernatural drink."

He who comes into contact with some share of its
treasure should not think that the only thing contained in
the word is what he himself has found. He should realize
that he has only been able to find that one thing from
among many others. Nor, because only that one part has
become his, should he say that the word is void and empty
and look down on it; but because he could not exhaust it
he should give thanks for its riches. Be glad that you were
overcome and do not be sad that it overcame you. The
thirsty man rejoices when he drinks and he is not down-
cast because he cannot empty the fountain. Rather let the
fountain quench your thirst than have your thirst quench
the fountain. Because if your thirst is quenched and the
fountain is not exhausted, you can drink from it again
whenever you are thirsty.

— ST. EPHRAEM THE SYRIAN (C. 306–73)

The Soul's Cry

O Jesu! tonight,
Thou Shepherd of the poor,
Thou sinless person
Who didst suffer full sore,
By ban of the wicked,

And wast crucified.
Save me from evil,
Save me from harm,
Save Thou my body,
Sanctify me tonight,
O Jesu! tonight,
Nor leave me.

Endow me with strength,
Thou Herdsman of might,
Guide me aright,
Guide me in Thy strength,
O Jesu! in Thy strength
Preserve me.

— TRADITIONAL CELTIC BLESSING
(C. 500 – C. 800)

Life Is in His Will

The first step in contemplation, dearly beloved, is to consider steadily what God wants, what is pleasing to him, what is acceptable in his sight. And since we all make many mistakes and the boldness of our will revolts against the rightness of his, and since the two cannot be brought into agreement and made to fit together, let us humble ourselves under the mighty hand of the most high God. In the sight of his mercy, let us take pains to show how in all things we stand in need of his mercy, saying: "Heal me, O Lord, and I shall be healed; save me and I shall be saved," and, "O Lord, be gracious to me, heal me, for I have sinned against you."

Once the eye of our heart has been cleansed by dwelling on thoughts of this kind, we are no longer left in bitterness in our own spirit, but we have great joy in the Spirit of God. We do not now consider what is God's will for us, but what God's will is, in itself.

"Life is in his will." Hence we may be sure that what is in harmony with his will is both useful and beneficial for us. It follows that we must take as much care never to deviate from that will as we do to preserve the life of our soul.

— ST. BERNARD OF CLAIRVAUX (1090–1153)

The Dart of Longing Love

But now you put me a question and say: "How might I think of him in himself, and what is he?" And to this I can only answer thus: "I have no idea." For with your question you have brought me into that same darkness, into that same cloud of unknowing where I would you were yourself. For a man may, by grace, have the fullness of knowledge of all other creatures and their works, yes, and of the works of God's own self, and he is well able to reflect on them. But no man can think of God himself. Therefore, it is my wish to leave everything that I can think of and choose for my love the thing that I cannot think. Because he can certainly be loved, but not thought. He can be taken and held by love but not by thought. Therefore, though it is good at times to think of the kindness and worthiness of God in particular, and though this is a light and a part of contemplation, nevertheless, in this exercise, it must be cast down and covered over with a cloud of forgetting. You are to step above it stalwartly but lovingly, and with a devout, pleasing, impulsive love strive to pierce that darkness above you. You are to smite upon that thick cloud of unknowing with a sharp dart of longing love. Do not leave that work for anything that may happen.

— FROM *THE CLOUD OF UNKNOWING*
(FOURTEENTH CENTURY)

The Name of Jesus

If you wish to be on good terms with God, and have his grace direct your life, and come to the joy of love, then fix this name "Jesus" so firmly in your heart that it never leaves your thought. And when you speak to him using your customary name "Jesu," in your ear it will be joy, in your mouth honey, and in your heart melody, because it will seem joy to you to hear that name being pronounced, sweetness to speak it, cheer and singing to think it.

— RICHARD ROLLE (C. 1300 – 49)

Jesus Is Near

Blessed be Jesus, who is always near in times of stress. Even when we cannot feel his presence he is close.

Jesus said within my heart, "I will never leave you either in happiness or distress. I will always be there to help you and watch over you. Nothing in heaven or earth can part you from me.

"When you are quiet and still I can speak to your heart."

— MARGERY KEMPE (C. 1373 – AFTER 1433)

Prayer of the Heart

We make our recollection in God because we long for him, and we long for him so that we may be recollected— so the one helps the other, and both arise from holy thoughts. You should therefore seek after God by short but ardent efforts of your heart.

Wonder at his beauty, invoke his aid, cast yourself in spirit at the foot of the cross, adore his goodness, speak frequently to him about your salvation; hold out your hand to him as a child to his father, that he may guide you. In every way excite your heart to the love of God.

This prayer is not difficult to practice. It can be interwoven with all our business and occupations without hindering them in the slightest degree. Indeed, our external pursuits are helped rather than hindered by our recollection and short ejaculations from the heart.

There are many useful collections of short vocal prayers, but I advise you not to confine yourself to any formal words. It is better to use those which are prompted by the feelings of your heart, as you need them. They will never fail you. But some surpass others, like the various invocations of the name of Jesus.

— ST. FRANCIS DE SALES (1567–1622)

No Grace without Suffering

The Lord, our Savior, raised his voice and spoke with incomparable majesty. "Let all know," he said, "that after sorrow grace follows; let them understand that without the burden of affliction one cannot arrive at the height of glory; that the measure of heavenly gifts is increased in proportion to the labors undertaken. Let them be on their guard against error or deception; this is the only ladder by which paradise is reached; without the cross there is no road to heaven."

When I heard these words I felt a great impulse to rush out into the street and shout at the top of my voice to everybody, no matter what their age, sex, or condition; "Listen, all you people; listen, all you nations. By Christ's command, using the very words that he uttered, I tell you most solemnly: no grace without suffering. Labor must be heaped upon labor to plumb the depths of the divine nature, the glory of the sons of God and the perfect happiness of the soul." . . .

No one would complain about the cross or about hardships coming seemingly by chance upon him, if he realized in what balance they are weighed before being distributed to men.

— ST. ROSE OF LIMA (1586 –1617)

Peace of Heart

Do you find that you are making no progress in prayer? Let it be enough for you to offer to God the prayer that our Savior makes for us in the most holy sacrament of the altar, using his fervent offering to make reparation for your own lukewarmness. And whenever you do anything, pray in this way: "My God, I am going to do this or endure that in the sacred heart of your divine Son and according to his holy intentions, which I offer you to make reparation for whatever evil or imperfection there may be in my own deeds."

Continue in this way in all the circumstances of life. And whenever anything happens to you that is painful, hard to hear, or mortifying, tell yourself this: "Accept what the Sacred Heart of Jesus sends you in order to unite you to himself."

But above all things maintain peace of heart that surpasses every treasure. For maintaining this peace, nothing is more effective than to renounce one's own will and to set in its place the will of the Sacred Heart, so that he may do for us whatever redounds to his glory and that we may joyfully submit to him and place in him our full confidence.

— ST. MARGARET MARY ALACOQUE (1647–90)

In the Presence of God

As you are less busy than others, employ more of your time in reading good books, and in order to make this more efficacious, set about it in this way:

Begin by placing yourself in the presence of God and by begging his help.

Read quietly, slowly, word for word, to enter into the subject more with the heart than with the mind.

At the end of each paragraph that contains a complete meaning, stop for the time it would take you to recite an Our Father, or even a little longer, to assimilate what you have read, or to rest and remain peacefully before God. Should this peace and rest last for a longer time, it will be all the better; but when you feel that your mind wanders, resume your reading, and continue thus, frequently renewing these same pauses.

Nothing need prevent you from continuing the same method, if you find it useful to your soul, during the time you have fixed for meditation.

— JEAN-PIERRE DE CAUSSADE (1675–1751)

Foretaste of Heaven

My children, your hearts are small, but prayer enlarges them and renders them capable of loving God. Prayer is a foretaste of heaven, an overflowing of heaven. It never leaves us without sweetness; it is like honey, it descends into the soul and sweetens everything. In a prayer well made, troubles vanish like snow under the rays of the sun.

Prayer makes time seem to pass quickly, and so pleasantly that one fails to notice how long it is. When I was parish priest of Bresse, once almost all my colleagues were ill, and as I made long journeys I used to pray to God, and, I assure you, the time did not seem long to me. There are those who lose themselves in prayer, like a fish in water, because they are absorbed in God. There is no division in their hearts. How I love those noble souls. St. Francis of Assisi and St. Colette saw our Lord and spoke to him as we speak to one another.

As for ourselves, how often do we come to church without thinking what we are going to do or for what we are going to ask.

And yet, when we go to call upon someone, we have no difficulty in remembering why it was we came. Some appear as if they were about to say to God: "I am just going to say a couple of words, so I can get away quickly." I often think that when we come to adore our Lord we should get all we ask if we asked for it with a lively faith and a pure heart.

— ST. JEAN-BAPTISTE VIANNEY (1786 –1859)

How to Pray

The power of prayer is indeed wonderful. It is like a queen, who, having free access always to the king, can obtain whatever she asks. To secure a hearing there is no need to recite set prayers composed for the occasion—were this the case, I should indeed deserve to be pitied!

Apart from the Office [the daily prayer of the church], which is a daily joy, I do not have the courage to search through books for beautiful prayers. They are so numerous that it would only make my head ache. Unable either to say them all or to choose between them, I do as a child would who cannot read—I just say what I want to say to God, quite simply, and he never fails to understand.

For me, prayer is an uplifting of the heart, a glance toward heaven, a cry of gratitude and love in times of sorrow as well as joy. It is something noble, something supernatural, which expands the soul and unites it to God.

When my state of spiritual aridity is such that not a single good thought will come, I repeat very slowly the Our Father and the Hail Mary, which are enough to console me and provide food for my soul.

— ST. THÉRÈSE OF LISIEUX (1873 – 97)

No Other Creature

Lord, my God, you have asked everything of your servant; take and receive everything, then. This day I belong to you without any reservations, forever. O Beloved of my soul! It is you only whom I want, and for your love I renounce all.

O God of Love! Take my memory and all its memories, take my intelligence so that it will act only for your greatest glory; take my will entirely, so that it will forever be drowned in your own; never again what I want, O most sweet Jesus, but always what you want; receive me, guide me, sanctify me, direct me; to you I abandon myself.

O God of all goodness, take my body and all its senses, my spirit and all its faculties, my heart and all its affections; O adorable Savior, you are the sole owner of my soul and of all my being; receive the immolation, that every day and every hour, I offer you in silence; deign to accept it and change it into graces and blessings for all those I love, for the conversion of sinners, and for the sanctification of souls.

O Jesus! Take all of my heart; it begs and sighs to belong to you alone; hold it always in your powerful hands so that it will surrender and pour itself out on no other creature.

Lord, take and sanctify all my words, my actions, my desires. Be for my soul its good and its all. To you I give and abandon it.

— MARTHE ROBIN (1902 – 81)

Maranatha (Come, Lord Jesus)

Reciting the mantra brings us to stillness and to peace. We recite it for as long as we need to before we are caught up into the prayer of Jesus. The general rule is that we must first learn to say it for the entire period of our meditation each morning and each evening, and then to allow it to do its work of calming over a period of years.

A day will come when the mantra ceases to sound and we become lost in the eternal silence of God. The rule when this happens is not to possess this silence or to use it for one's own satisfaction.

As soon as we consciously realize that we are in this profound silence and then begin to reflect about it we must gently and quietly return to our mantra.

Gradually the silences become longer and we are simply absorbed in the mystery of God. The important thing is to have the courage and generosity to return to the mantra as soon as we become self-conscious of the silence.

Each of us is summoned to the heights of Christian prayer, to the fullness of life. What we need, however, is the humility to tread the way very faithfully over a period of years so that the prayer of Christ may indeed be the grounding experience of life.

—JOHN MAIN (1926 – 82)

MYSTICAL PRAYER

My lover speaks; he says to me,
"Arise, my beloved, my beautiful one,
and come!
For see, the winter is past,
the rains are over and gone.
The flowers appear on the earth,
the time of pruning the vines has come,
and the song of the dove is heard in our land.
The fig tree puts forth its figs,
and the vines, in bloom, give forth fragrance.
Arise, my beloved, my beautiful one,
and come!"

—SONG OF SONGS 2:10–13

Enlighten Our Eyes

Come now, insignificant man, fly for a moment from your affairs, escape for a little while from the tumult of your thoughts. Put aside now your weighty cares and leave your wearisome toils. Abandon yourself for a little to God and rest for a little in him.

Enter into the inner chamber of your soul, shut out everything save God and what can be of help in your quest for him, and having locked the door, seek him out. Speak now, my whole heart, speak now to God: "I seek your countenance, O Lord, your countenance I seek."

Come then, Lord my God, teach my heart where and how to seek you, where and how to find you.

Lord, if you are not present here, where, since you are absent, shall I look for you? On the other hand, if you are everywhere, why then, since you are present, do I not see you? But surely you dwell in light inaccessible. And where is this inaccessible light, or how can I approach the inaccessible light? Or who shall lead me and take me into it that I may see you in it? Again, by what signs, under what aspect, shall I seek you? Never have I seen you, Lord my God, I do not know your face.

———•———

What shall he do, most high Lord, what shall this exile do, far away from you as he is? What shall your servant do, tormented by love of you and yet cast off far from your face? He yearns to see you, and your countenance is too far away from him. He desires to come close to you, and your dwelling place is inaccessible; he longs to find you and does not know where you are; he is eager to seek you out and he does not know your countenance.

Lord, you are my God and my Lord, and never have I seen you. You have created me and re-created me and you have given me all the good things I possess, and still I do not know you. In fine, I was made in order to see you, and I have not yet accomplished what I was made for.

And you, O Lord, how long? How long, Lord, will you be unmindful of us? How long will you turn your countenance from us? When will you look upon us and hear us? When will you enlighten our eyes and show your countenance to us? When will you give yourself again to us?

Look upon us, Lord; hear us, enlighten us, show yourself to us. Give yourself to us that it may be well with us, for without you it goes so ill for us. Have pity upon our efforts and our strivings toward you, for we can avail nothing without you.

Teach me to seek you, and reveal yourself to me as I seek, because I can neither seek you if you do not teach me how, nor find you unless you reveal yourself. Let me seek you in desiring you; let me desire you in seeking you; let me find you in loving you; let me love you in finding you.

— St. Anselm of Canterbury (c. 1033–1109)

Love Is Its Own Reward

Love is self-sufficient; it is pleasing to itself and on its own account. Love is its own payment, its own reward. Love needs no extrinsic cause or result. Love is the result of love, it is intrinsically valuable. I love because I love; I love in order to love. Love is a valuable thing only if it returns to its beginning, consults its origin, and flows back to its source. It must always draw from that endless stream. Love is the only one of the soul's motions, senses, and affections by which the creature in his inadequate fashion may respond to his Creator and pay him back in kind. When God loves, he wishes only to be loved in return; assuredly he loves for no other purpose than to be loved. He knows that those who love him are happy in their love.

The Bridegroom's love, that Bridegroom who is himself love, seeks only reciprocal love and loyalty. She who is loved may well love in return! How can the bride not love, the very bride of Love? Why should Love itself not be loved?

—— • ——

The bride, duly renouncing all other affections, submits with all her being to love alone; she can respond to love by giving love in return. When she has poured forth her whole being in love, how does her effort compare with the unending flow from the very source of love? Love itself of course is more abundant than a lover, the Word than a created soul, the Bridegroom than the bride, the Creator than the creature. As well compare a thirsty man with the fountain that satisfies his thirst!

Can it be that all will perish and come to nought, the promised love of the bride, the longing of the creature here below, the passion of the lover, the confidence of the believer, simply because it is futile to race against a giant, or to contend with honey in sweetness, with the lamb in gentleness, with the lily in whiteness, with the sun in splendor, with Love in love? Not at all. Even though the creature loves less than the Creator, for that is his nature, nevertheless if he loves with all his being, he lacks nothing. One who so loves, therefore, has indeed become a bride; for she cannot so offer love and not be loved in return: in the agreement of the partners lies the wholeness and the perfection of marriage. Who can doubt that the Word's love for the soul is prior to, and greater than, the soul's love for him?

— ST. BERNARD OF CLAIRVAUX (1090–1153)

Make Room for Christ

Many are his visits to the man of inward life. With such a one he holds delightful converse, granting him sweet comfort, much peace, and an intimacy astonishing beyond measure.

Come then, faithful soul, prepare your heart for this your Spouse, so that he may vouchsafe to come to you and dwell within you.

For so he says: "If any man love me, he will keep my word; and we will come to him and make our dwelling with him."

Make room therefore for Christ, and refuse entrance to all others.

When you have Christ, you are rich and have need of nought else.

He will provide for you, and be in all things your faithful procurator; you shall not need to look to men.

Put your whole trust in God; let him be your fear and your love.

— THOMAS À KEMPIS (C. 1380–1471)

Angelic Dart

It pleased the Lord that I should sometimes see the following vision. I would see beside me, on my left hand, an angel in bodily form—a type of vision that I am not in the habit of seeing, except very rarely. Though I often see representations of angels, my visions of them are of the type that I first mentioned. It pleased the Lord that I should see this angel in the following way. He was not tall, but short, and very beautiful, his face so aflame that he appeared to be one of the highest types of angel who seem to be all afire. They must be those who are called cherubim: they do not tell me their names but I am well aware that there is a great difference between certain angels and others, and between these and others still, of a kind that I could not possibly explain. In his hands I saw a long golden spear and at the end of the iron tip I seemed to see a point of fire. With this he seemed to pierce my heart several times so that it penetrated to my entrails. When he drew it out, I thought he was drawing them out with it, and he left me completely afire with a great love of God. The pain was so sharp that it made me utter several moans; and so excessive was the sweetness caused me by this intense pain that one can never wish to lose it, nor will one's soul be content with anything less than God. It is not bodily pain, but spiritual, though the body has a share in it—indeed a great share. So sweet are the colloquies of love that pass between the soul and God that if anyone thinks I am lying I beseech God, in His Goodness, to give him the same experience.

—ST. TERESA OF ÁVILA (1515 – 82)

Dark Night

So dark the night! At rest
and hushed my house, I went with no one knowing
upon a lover's quest
—Ah the sheer grace!—so blest,
my eager heart with love aflame and glowing.

In darkness, hid from sight
I went by secret ladder safe and sure
—Ah grace of sheer delight!—
so softly veiled by night,
hushed now my house, in darkness and secure.

Hidden in that glad night,
regarding nothing as I stole away,
no one to see my flight,
no other guide or light
save one that in my heart burned bright as day.

Surer than noonday sun,
guiding me from the start this radiant light
led me to that dear One
waiting for me, well-known,
somewhere apart where no one came in sight.

— • —

Dark of the night, my guide,
fairer by far than dawn when stars grow dim!
Night that has unified
the Lover and the Bride,
transforming the Beloved into him.

There on my flowered breast
that none but he might ever own or keep,

he stayed, sinking to rest,
and softly I caressed
my Love while cedars gently fanned his sleep.

Breeze from the turret blew
ruffling his hair. Then with his tranquil hand
wounding my neck, I knew
nothing: my senses flew
at touch of peace too deep to understand.

Forgetting all, my quest
ended, I stayed lost to myself at last.
All ceased: my face was pressed
upon my Love, at rest,
with all my cares among the lilies cast.

— ST. JOHN OF THE CROSS (1542 – 91)

Her Unique Spouse

It was on the day of the Annunciation, the twenty-fifth of
March 1679, at eight o'clock in the morning, that Kateri
Tekakwitha a moment after Jesus Christ had been given to
her in Holy Communion, gave herself also entirely to
Him, and renouncing marriage forever, promised to Him
her perpetual virginity, and finally with a heart on fire with
love called on Him to deign to be her unique spouse, and
to take herself as His spouse in return. She prayed Our
Lady that Our Lady might with tender devotion present
her to her Divine Son; then wishing to make a double sacrifice in a single act, she at the same time as she gave herself devout to Jesus Christ, consecrated herself wholly to

Mary begging her to be from then on her mother, and to take her as her daughter.
(Blessed Kateri Tekakwitha: 1656–80)

— FATHER CHOLENEC

Interior Priesthood

As I was plunged in the most profound recollection, uniting myself to the Divine Victim for the glory of his Father, I felt myself in the inmost depths of my soul, penetrated by the presence of Jesus within me. He let me hear words (in a language other than ours) that ravished me with love and bliss. He promised me an ever increasing intimate union with his immolation—a continuous participation, if I so wished, in the adorable Sacrifice continually offered.

He made me understand that there is an intimate and universal priesthood, absolutely and necessarily united to his, which should be the portion of all souls, but which is so of only very few. This priesthood is wholly interior, and is only granted to a soul who consents to it, who has desired it, and who to obtain it wills to immolate itself at all times with Jesus; that even so, in reality it is not the soul who immolates itself but Jesus who immolates it with himself. But as the soul wills to be immolated and abandons itself for that purpose, Jesus makes it participate in his state of victim and priesthood at one and the same time. He consecrates it and ordains it to an interior priesthood that conforms it to his Eucharistic life more than any other gift it has received. This priesthood communicates to the soul a far more perfect grace of union in view of being immolated to the glory of God, thereby rendering infinite honor to God the Father, since it is no longer separated from the Divine Lamb.

— MARIE-ADELE GARNIER (1838–1924)

Descent to Simplicity

Imagine a man of forty. His Mother is still alive; he loves and respects her and each day faithfully he visits her and spends half an hour in her company. He does this in spite of a busy and increasingly demanding professional and family life. They talk of this and that and when the half hour is over, he leaves—to return the next day. What more could a Mother ask?

This represents the beginning of a life of prayer. Each day a set time is spent on meditation and a method is faithfully followed point by point. This is a beginning, it is something . . . but one might sometimes think, from what they say, that those who set time aside in this way for prayer are doing wonders!

But if this soul is faithful in prayer and God draws him closer, he will become surprisingly younger! No longer the man of forty spending the dutiful half hour with his Mother but a young man of twenty who lives away from home, has his own friends and interests. But he comes back often and spends long hours with his family. And the soul grows younger still: a youngster of fifteen is still living at home and feels the security of his parent's house. Our heavenly Father grants to the soul the request of the psalmist to "live in the house of the Lord all the days of his life." The house of the Lord is the house of prayer. It is not a matter of continually speaking to God or of God, but rather that the eyes of the soul are continually on God, all action is initiated by God, God seems to envelop the soul. What extraordinary progress this is: not to be able to leave God.

— • —

As the soul moves along the path of prayer he can be compared to a child of ten whose conversation is not yet that of an adult, and his Mother loves his sayings just because of this. If we continue to move "forward" we find a child of two years old or so. An age at which Mother and child can each fill the world of the other. The child's babbling is incomprehensible to any but his Mother, who knows and understands. His Mother becomes small for his sake, to babble with him.

We should indeed be surprised if we heard a recording of the prayer of the saints. We would be surprised by their simplicity, their childlikeness, their stammerings of love. This extreme simplicity is necessary to them as a means of holding fast to God in the midst of their work, their suffering and difficulties. God suffices—and here is a strange thing—the saints suffice for God. . . . When a Mother is listening to her young child, does she notice what goes on around her? And so it is with God. All the iniquities of men, all the blasphemies are no longer heard. God does not punish; he is with his saints and hears only their childlike words and it is these words that bring us mercy.

— • —

But we must carry the comparison further. A baby does not talk or walk but depends entirely on his Mother; he is moved in her arms. This age is that of great saints. They are lost in God and no longer able to talk, a sacred silence, more telling than the babbling of childhood. These great saints can live only on God, they depend on him utterly, as a young infant depends on his Mother. The great saints cannot leave God.

Is that as far as we can go? Surely the greatest union between Mother and child is before birth? He is one with her. We do not see him; he lives in her.

Thus, the greatest saints, the closest to God. One no longer sees them, for they seem lost, melted into God, having no other life than the life they share with him. They seem dead and yet they live a mysterious, intimate life with God. This is the life of which St. Paul spoke when he said, "We are dead and our life is hidden in God."

— THOMAS DEHAU (1870 –1956)

Dryness in Prayer

You may think that I am exaggerating the night of my soul. If one judged by the poems I have composed this year, it might seem that I have been inundated with consolation, that I am a child for whom the veil of faith is almost rent asunder. . . . But it is not a veil. . . . It is a wall that reaches to the very heavens, shutting out the starry sky.

When I sing in my verses of the happiness of heaven and of the eternal possession of God, I feel no joy. I sing out of what I wish to believe. Sometimes, I confess, a feeble ray of sunshine penetrates my dark night and brings me a moment's relief, but after it has gone, the remembrance of it, instead of consoling me, makes the blackness seem denser still.

And yet I have never experienced more fully the sweetness and mercy of the Lord. He did not send this heavy cross when it would, I believe, have discouraged me, but chose a time when I was able to bear it. Now it does no more than deprive me of all natural satisfaction in my longing for heaven.

— ST. THÉRÈSE OF LISIEUX (1873 – 97)

A Mystical Heart

Many mystics tell us that, in addition to the mind and heart with which we ordinarily communicate with God, we are, all of us, endowed with a mystical mind and mystical heart, a faculty that makes it possible for us to know God directly, to grasp and intuit him in his very being, though in a dark manner, apart from all thoughts and concepts and images.

Ordinarily all our contact with God is indirect— through images and concepts that necessarily distort his reality. To be able to grasp him beyond these thoughts and images is the privilege of this faculty that, in the course of this explanation, I shall call the Heart (a word dear to the author of *The Cloud of Unknowing*) though it has nothing to do with our physical heart or our affectivity.

In most of us this Heart lies dormant and undeveloped. If it were to be awakened it would be constantly straining toward God and, given a chance, would impel the whole of our being toward him. But for this, it needs to be developed, it needs to have the dross that surrounds it removed so that it can be attracted toward the Eternal Magnet.

— ANTHONY DE MELLO (1931– 87)

TAKING THE RISK: THE JOURNEY TO GOD

The life of a Christian is properly described as a journey, or perhaps a story, with a beginning, a middle, and an end. The beginning is an act of conversion, a personal trans- formation in response to God's grace and love. Conversion leads to changed behavior. Christians find a growing con- viction that their life has a purpose. This sense of vocation has both a general and a particular meaning. In the gen- eral sense, Christians are called by Christ to follow him and to become signs of and witnesses to the reign of God in the world. Most Christians are called to a specific state in life—to marry, to join a religious vocation, or to live single. Each leads to a particular manner of living that in- volves different responsibilities, specific tasks, and unique opportunities to build the body of Christ and to witness to God's love.

CONVERSION AND CALL

A s he was walking by the Sea of Galilee, he saw two brothers, Simon who is called Peter, and his brother Andrew, casting a net into the sea; they were fishermen. He said to them, "Come after me, and I will make you fishers of men." At once they left their nets and followed him. He walked along from there and saw two other brothers, James, the son of Zebedee, and his brother John. They were in a boat, with their father Zebedee, mending their nets. He called them, and immediately they left their boat and their father and followed him.

—MATTHEW 4:18–22

The Calling of St. Anthony of Egypt

After the death of his parents, Anthony was left alone with an only sister, who was very young. He was about eighteen or twenty years old, and undertook the care of the household and his sister.

Less than six months had passed after the death of his parents, and he was going to the church, as was his custom, turning over in his mind the way that the apostles had left everything to follow the Savior, and also how those people in the Acts of the Apostles had sold their possessions and had laid the proceeds at the feet of the apostles for distribution among the needy. He was also thinking of the great hope stored up in heaven for these people. With these things in his mind, he went into the church. It happened that the gospel was then being read, and he heard what the Lord had said to the rich man: "If you would be perfect, go, sell what you possess and give to the poor, and you will have treasure in heaven; and come, follow me."

As though this reminder of the saints had been sent to him by God, and as though that passage had been read specially for his sake, Anthony went out immediately, and gave to the villagers the possessions he had inherited from his ancestors—they consisted of some three hundred very pleasant and fertile acres—so that they would not be an encumbrance to him and to his sister. He sold all his possessions and gave the considerable sum he raised to the poor, keeping back only a little of it for his sister.

———•———

Again when he went into church, he heard what the Lord said in the gospel: "Do not be anxious about tomorrow." He could not wait any longer, but went out and gave away even what he had kept back to the poor. He left his sister in the care of some well-known, trustworthy virgins, putting her in a convent to be brought up, and he devoted himself to the ascetic life not far from his home, living in recollection and practicing self-denial.

He labored with his own hands, for he had heard that "if anyone will not work, let him not eat." And of what he earned, part he spent on food, and part he gave to the poor.

He prayed frequently, for he had learned that one ought to pray in secret, and pray without ceasing. He was so careful in his reading of scripture that nothing escaped him, but he retained it all; so that afterward his memory served him in place of books.

And so all the people of the village, and the good men with whom he associated saw what kind of man he was, and they called him "the friend of God." Some loved him as a son, and others as though he were a brother. *(St. Anthony of Egypt: c. 251–356)*

— ST. ATHANASIUS (D. 373)

Reluctant Archbishop

Anselm, with some misgiving, came over to visit a sick friend in England at a time when the archbishopric of Canterbury had long been left vacant, so that King William Rufus and his creatures might enjoy the sequestrated revenues of the See. At Christmas 1092, the clergy were allowed to pray for a remedy for the misfortunes of the Church. Early in 1093 King William fell sick and was evidently at the point of death; fortunately for himself, the Norman king was more prompt in seeing the point of the situation. He promised amendment and restitution of every possible kind, and sent for Anselm at once as the obvious person to be elected archbishop.

And then began a scene that has been enacted with various results a thousand times in the history of sanctity, but seldom with so much publicity or so much dramatic interest as in St. Anselm's case. When you try to make a saint accept a bishopric, it is like trying to make a child take medicine; the result is a perfect fury of dissent. In this case not merely the ordinary considerations but the whole welfare of a long-widowed Church and, as seemed probable, the life of a notorious sinner were depending upon St. Anselm's acceptance, and he simply refused. It was only by the use of physical force that they dragged the saint to the King's bedside: and there, pressing the crosier against the knuckles that would not open so as to hold it, they elected the Archbishop of Canterbury.

(St. Anselm of Canterbury: c. 1033–1109)

— RONALD KNOX (1888 –1957)

Test the Spirits

Ignatius was very addicted to reading aimless and exaggerated books about the illustrious deeds of the famous, and when he felt well again he asked for some to pass the time. But there were no books of that type in the house and he was given a book called *The Life of Christ* and another *The Flower of the Saints,* both in his native language.

By reading these regularly he developed a certain sympathy with what was written in them. Sometimes he took his mind off them and turned his thoughts to the type of story he used to read earlier on; sometimes, according as it occurred to him, he thought about those idle inclinations, and things of that nature, such as he used to think about formerly.

But divine mercy was at hand, and in place of these thoughts, it used to substitute others from what he had recently read. For when he had read the lives of Christ our Lord and the saints he would think to himself and ponder:

"What if I were to do what blessed Francis did or what blessed Dominic did?" And he used to meditate a good deal in this manner. This way of thinking lasted for some time, but then other things intervened, and he resumed his idle and worldly thoughts, and these persisted for a long time. He was involved in that succession of changes of mind for a considerable time.

— • —

But there was a difference in his two types of subject for thought. When he was intent on his worldly interests he got great pleasure at the time, but whenever he wearied of them and gave them up, he felt dejected and empty. On the other hand, when he thought about the austerities that he found that holy men practiced, not only did he find joy in the account of them, but when he stopped thinking of them his joy remained unabated. However, he never noticed the difference or thought about it, until one day it dawned on him, and he began to wonder at it. He understood from experience that the one subject of thought left him dejection, while the other left him joy. This was the first conclusion that he reached concerning things of a supernatural nature. Afterward, however, when he had undertaken spiritual exercises, this experience was the starting point for teaching his followers the discernment of spirits.
(St. Ignatius of Loyola: 1491–1556)

Thy Will in Me

O Parent of parents and Friend of all friends,
Thy intent in thus disposing was different from this;

For here without entreaty thou tookest me into thy care,
And by degrees led me from all else
That at length I might see and settle my love in thee.
What had I ever done to please thee?
Or what was there in me wherewith to serve thee?
Much less could I ever deserve to be chosen by thee.
O happy begun freedom the beginning of all my good,
And more worth to me at that time than the whole
   world besides.
Had I never since hindered thy will and working in me
What degrees of grace should I now have had!
It is more than nineteen years since and where as yet
   am I?
   My Jesus, forgive me,
   Remember what thou hast done for me
   And whither thou hast brought me,
   And for this excess of goodness and love
   Let me no more hinder thy will in me.

— MARY WARD (1585–1645)

Created for Service

God has created me to do Him some definite service;
He has committed some work to me which He has not
   committed to another.
I have my mission—I may never know it in this life,
but I shall be told it in the next.
I am a link in a chain, a bond of connection between
   persons.
He has not created me for nothing. I shall do good.
   I shall do His work.

I shall be an angel of peace, a preacher of truth in my
   own place,
if I do but keep His commandments.
Therefore, I will trust Him.
Whatever, wherever I am. I can never be thrown away.
If I am in sickness, my sickness may serve Him.
In perplexity, my perplexity may serve Him;
if I am in sorrow, my sorrow may serve Him.
He does nothing in vain. He knows what he is about.
He may take away my friends, throw me among
   strangers.
He may make me feel desolate, make my spirits sink,
   hide my future from me,
still He knows what He is about.

—VENERABLE JOHN HENRY NEWMAN (1801–90)

The Hound of Heaven

I fled Him, down the nights and down the days;
   I fled Him, down the arches of the years;
I fled Him, down the labyrinthine ways
   Of my own mind; and in the mist of tears
I hid from Him, and under running laughter.
         Up vistaed hopes, I sped;
         And shot, precipitated,
Adown Titanic glooms of chasmèd fears,
   From those strong Feet that followed, followed after.

         But with unhurrying chase,
         And unperturbèd pace,
Deliberate speed, majestic instancy,
         They beat—and a Voice beat

More instant than the Feet—
"All things betray thee, who betrayest Me." . . .

Now of that long pursuit
Comes on at hand the bruit;
That Voice is round me like a bursting sea:
"And is thy earth so marred,
Shattered in shard on shard?
Lo, all things fly thee, for thou fliest Me!
Strange, piteous, futile thing,
Wherefore should any set thee love apart?
Seeing none but I makes much of naught?" (He said),
"And human love needs human meriting:
How hast thou merited—
Of all man's clotted clay the dingiest clot?
Alack, thou knowest not
How little worthy of any love thou art!
Whom wilt thou find to love ignoble thee,
Save Me, save only Me?
All which I took from thee I did but take,
Not for thy harms,
But just that thou might'st seek it in My arms.
All which thy child's mistake
Fancies as lost, I have stored for thee at home:
Rise, clasp My hand, and come."

Halts by me that footfall:
Is my gloom, after all,
Shade of His hand, outstretched caressingly?
"Ah, fondest, blindest, weakest,
I am He Whom thou seekest!
Thou dravest love from thee, who dravest Me."

— FRANCIS THOMPSON (1859–1907)

My Vocation Is Love

All the gifts of heaven, even the most perfect of them, without love, are absolutely nothing; charity is the best way of all, because it leads straight to God. . . . When St. Paul was talking about the different members of the mystical body I couldn't recognize myself in any of them; or rather I could recognize myself in all of them. But charity—that was the key to my vocation. If the Church was a body composed of different members, it couldn't lack the noblest of all; it must have a heart, and a heart burning with love. And I realized that this love was the true motive force that enabled the other members of the Church to act; if it ceased to function the apostles would forget to preach the gospel, the martyrs would refuse to shed their blood. Love, in fact, is the vocation that includes all others; it's a universe of its own, comprising all time and space—it's eternal. Beside myself with joy, I cried out: "Jesus, my love! I've found my vocation, and my vocation is love." I had discovered where it is that I belong in the Church, the niche God has appointed for me. To be nothing else than love, deep down in the heart of Mother Church; that's to be everything at once—my dream wasn't a dream after all.

— ST. THÉRÈSE OF LISIEUX (1873 – 97)

Beauty and Joy

Mrs. Barrett gave me my first impulse toward Catholicism. It was around ten o'clock in the morning that I went up to Kathryn's to call for her to come out and play. There was no one on the porch or in the kitchen. The breakfast dishes had all been washed. They were long railroad apartments, those flats, and thinking the children must be in the front room, I burst in and ran through the bedrooms.

In the front room Mrs. Barrett was on her knees, saying her prayers. She turned to tell me that Kathryn and the children had all gone to the store and went on with her praying. And I felt a warm burst of love toward Mrs. Barrett that I have never forgotten, a feeling of gratitude and happiness that still warms my heart when I remember her. She had God, and there was beauty and joy in her life.

All through my life what she was doing remained with me. And though I became oppressed with the problem of poverty and injustice, though I groaned at the hideous sordidness of man's lot, though there were years when I clung to the philosophy of economic determination as an explanation of man's fate, still there were moments when in the midst of misery and class strife, life was shot through with glory. Mrs. Barrett in her sordid little tenement flat finished her breakfast dishes at ten o'clock in the morning and got down on her knees and prayed to God.

— DOROTHY DAY (1897–1980)

Man of Hope

The monk leaves the world, retires to the wilderness, the forest, the mountains, the lonely shores of the sea: and there, descending by his prayer into the empty spaces of his own spirit, he waits for the fulfillment of the divine promises: "The land that was desolate and impassable shall be glad, and the wilderness shall rejoice and shall flourish like the lily" (Isaiah 35:1).

The monk is a man of sorrow, a man discontented with every illusion, aware of his own poverty, impatient of evasion, who seeks the naked realities that only the desert can reveal. But the monk is also a man of joy, a man at peace with the emptiness of the wilderness, glad of his limitations, loving reality as he finds it, and therefore secure in his humility. He is a man of joy and a man of sorrow both together because he is a man of desires. And because he lives by pure hope, he has entered into the secret that Christ has taught His chosen ones.

— THOMAS MERTON (1915 – 68)

STATES OF
LIFE

Try to learn what is pleasing to the Lord. Take no part in the fruitless works of darkness; rather expose them, for it is shameful even to mention the things done by them in secret; but everything exposed by the light becomes visible, for everything that becomes visible is light. Therefore, it says:

> *"Awake, O sleeper,*
>   *and arise from the dead,*
> *and Christ will give you light."*

Watch carefully then how you live, not as foolish persons but as wise, making the most of the opportunity, because the days are evil. Therefore, do not continue in ignorance, but try to understand what is the will of the Lord.

—EPHESIANS 5:10–17

A Bishop's Prayer

Christ my God, you humbled yourself in order to lift me, a straying sheep, onto your shoulders. You fed me in green pastures and nourished me with the waters of true doctrine by the hands of your shepherds. They, whom you yourself fed, afterward fed your elect and chosen flock.

Now you have called me, Lord, by the hands of your bishop to minister to your disciples. Why, indeed, in your providence you acted so, I do not know. You alone know that.

Lord, lighten the heavy burden of my sins by which I have seriously offended you. Cleanse my mind and my heart. Like a bright lamp, guide me along the right path.

Put the right word on my lips. Grant me a clear and ready tongue by the tongues of fire of your Holy Spirit that your presence may ever protect me.

Feed me, Lord, and feed with me, that my heart may not deviate either to right or left. Let your good Spirit guide me in the right way and may my works be in accordance with your will. Let it be so, right to the end.

— ST. JOHN OF DAMASCUS (C. 675 – C. 749)

Continual Prayer

The monk, who continues faithfully in his cell and lets himself be molded by it, will gradually find that his whole life tends to become one continual prayer. But he cannot attain to this repose except at the cost of stern battle; both by living austerely in fidelity to the law of the Cross, and willingly accepting the tribulations by which God will try him as gold in the furnace. In this way, having been cleansed in the night of patience, and having been consoled and sustained by assiduous meditation of the Scriptures, and having been led by the Holy Spirit into the depths of his own soul, he is now ready, not only to serve God, but even to cleave to him in love.

— ST. BRUNO HARTENFAUST (C. 1030 –1101)

St. Hugh of Lincoln, the Bishop-Elect

It was a gallant and bravely equipped escort that awaited the bishop-elect; knights and canons, with chaplains, squires, and servants to do honor to the king's friend, the bishop-elect of the great see of Lincoln. Only one person in the procession was but poorly arrayed and that was the bishop-elect himself. The shabbily dressed monk who rode in the midst of the canons was still a Carthusian, would be indeed a Carthusian till his death; he was not yet a bishop and therefore it did not behoove him to put off his habit.

They were put to shame, canons and knights, chaplains and squires and servants, the latter in especial, by the mean attire of the principal member of the cavalcade. And to make it worse the bishop-elect insisted on carrying a wretched bundle of sheepskins, tied to the saddlebow, which he said was his bedding. Of course while they were journeying through the country it did not matter so much how the bishop-elect was dressed, there was nobody to see him, and no one to comment on the horrible bundle. But it was too embarrassing when they came to towns and remarks were passed by irreverent burgesses. So just before the procession entered the city of Winchester, where royalty and nobles, it was said, would greet the bishop-elect, a certain chaplain managed to cut the strap that held the odious sheepskins to the saddlebow, and the offensive bundle fell to the ground. Hugh did not notice the loss; wrapped in meditation he was aware neither of the embarrassment he caused nor of the dexterous removal of his bedding.

(St. Hugh of Lincoln: c. 1140–1200)

— JOSEPH CLAYTON

The Holiness of St. Elizabeth of Hungary

Elizabeth's holiness began to come to its full flower. All her life she had been the comfort of the poor: now she became the helper of the starving. Outside one of her castles she built a hospice and gathered in it sick, diseased, and crippled men and women. Besides, anyone who came asking for alms received unstinted gifts from her charity. She did the same wherever her husband's jurisdiction ran, pouring out all the resources she had in all parts of his territories, until in the end she sold even her jewels and her sumptuous dresses.

She went twice a day to see the sick, in the early morning and at nightfall, and it was those with the foulest diseases she made her personal care. She fed them herself, made and cleaned their pallets, carried them in her arms, and nursed them in whatever way they needed. Her husband, of happy memory, gave a completely ungrudging consent to all she did. When he died she felt she should now attempt the heights of perfection. She came to me and begged me with tears to let her beg her way from door to door.

On the Good Friday of that year, after the altars had been stripped, she knelt in front of the altar of the chapel she had given to the Friars Minor and laid her hands on it. Then in their presence she renounced her own will, her earthly estate, and all that our Savior counsels us in the gospel to put aside.

(St. Elizabeth of Hungary: 1207–31)

— CONRAD OF MARBURG (C. 1180 –1233)

Inferno

Midway this way of life we're bound upon,
I woke to find myself in a dark wood,
Where the right road was wholly lost and gone.

Ay me! how hard to speak of it—that rude
And rough and stubborn forest! the mere breath
Of memory stirs the old fear in the blood;

It is so bitter, it goes nigh to death;
Yet there I gained such good, that, to convey
The tale, I'll write what else I found therewith.

How I got into it I cannot say,
Because I was so heavy and full of sleep
When first I stumbled from the narrow way;

But when at last I stood beneath a steep
Hill's side, which closed that valley's wandering maze
Whose dread had pierced me to the heart-root deep,

Then I looked up, and saw the morning rays
Mantle its shoulder from that planet bright
Which guides men's feet aright on all their ways.

— DANTE ALIGHIERI (1265–1321)

Being a Martha

His Majesty does not lead all souls by the same way. St.
Martha was holy, though we are never told she was a contemplative; would you not be content with resembling this
blessed woman who deserved to receive Christ our Lord

so often into her home, where she fed and served him, and where he ate at her table?

Imagine that this little community is the house of St. Martha where there must be different kinds of people. Remember that someone must cook the meals and count yourselves happy in being able to serve like Martha.

Reflect that true humility consists in being willing and ready to do what our Lord asks of us. It always makes us consider ourselves unworthy to be reckoned among his servants.

Then if contemplation, mental and vocal prayer, nursing the sick, the work of the house, and the most menial labor all serve this Guest, why should we choose to minister to him in one way rather than in another?

— ST. TERESA OF ÁVILA (1515 – 82)

Lawrence of the Resurrection

[Brother Lawrence said] that he was then happily employed in the cobbler's workshop; but that he was as ready to quit that post as the former, since he was always finding pleasure in every condition by doing little things for the love of God.

With him the set times of prayers were not different from other times.

He retired to pray, according to the direction of his Superior, but he did not want such retirement or ask for it, because his greatest business did not divert him from God.

As he knew his obligation to love God in all things, and as he endeavored so to do, he had no need of a director to advise him, but he needed much a confessor to absolve him.

He was very sensible of his faults, but not discouraged by them.

He confessed them to God, but did not plead against him to excuse them.

When he had done so, he peaceably resumed his usual practice of love and adoration.

(*Brother Lawrence: c. 1614–91*)

Growing Older

Lord, thou knowest better than I know myself that I am growing older and will someday be old. Keep me from the fatal habit of thinking I must say something on every subject and on every occasion. Release me from craving to straighten out everybody's affairs. Make me thoughtful but not moody: helpful but not bossy. With my vast store of wisdom, it seems a pity not to use it all, but thou knowest, Lord, that I want a few friends at the end. Keep my mind free from the recital of endless details; give me wings to get to the point. Seal my lips on my aches and pains. They are increasing, and love of rehearsing them is becoming sweeter as the years go by. I dare not ask for grace enough to enjoy the tales of others' pains, but help me to endure them with patience.

I dare not ask for improved memory, but for a growing humility and lessening cocksureness when my memory seems to clash with the memories of others. Teach me the glorious lesson that occasionally I may be mistaken. Keep me reasonably sweet; I do not want to be a saint—some of them are so hard to live with—but a sour old person is one of the crowning works of the devil. Give me the ability to see good things in unexpected places, and talents in unexpected people. And, give me, O Lord, the grace to tell them so.

— A SEVENTEENTH-CENTURY NUN

God Found Madeleine Delbrêl

When asked whether a Christian could live among atheists and keep the faith, Madeleine usually responded that to keep the faith as if guarding a fortress had nothing to do with real faith. She maintained that a person could become a better Christian living beside unbelievers because they provided the stimulus for a healthier and more authentic faith. Atheists tended to unmask the complacency of believers, which in other contexts remains forever masked. They made her aware that the silence of Christians often indicated apathy or ignorance. Therefore Christians were not hurt but helped when awakened from their dreamy indifference or shaken out of their stupor. . . .

Rather than well-recited words or a simple call for help, her prayer was a wordless cry for God that rose from the depths of her being. Madeleine later wrote that during days of intensive prayer she had felt not so much that she had found God but that God had found her. Through this prayer she also sensed that God had to remain her ultimate question and not her fixed answer, her all-encompassing mystery and not her limited possession. She was now

willing to accept God as greater and more profound than her former abyss.
(*Madeleine Delbrêl: 1904–64*)

— CHARLES F. MANN

Living as a Good Shepherd

The good shepherd is one who lays down his life for his people. Some live this calling literally, shedding their blood as martyrs. Others live it in the unstinting giving of their time, their energy, their very selves to those they have been called to serve. Whatever the future holds for me, I pledge this day to live as a good shepherd who willingly lays down his life for you.

— JOSEPH BERNARDIN (1928 – 96)

Joseph, Your Brother

As our lives and ministries are mingled together through the breaking of the Bread and the blessing of the Cup, I hope that long before my name falls from the eucharistic prayer in the silence of death you will know well who I am. You will know because we will work and play together, fast and pray together, mourn and rejoice together, despair and hope together, dispute and be reconciled together. You will know me as a friend, fellow priest, and bishop. You will know also that I love you. For I am Joseph, your brother!

— JOSEPH BERNARDIN (1928 – 96)

MARRIAGE

O n the third day there was a wedding in Cana
in Galilee, and the mother of Jesus was there.
Jesus and his disciples were also invited to the wedding. When the wine ran short, the mother of Jesus said
to him, "They have no wine." [And] Jesus said to her,
"Woman, how does your concern affect me? My hour
has not yet come." His mother said to the servers, "Do
whatever he tells you." Now there were six stone water
jars there for Jewish ceremonial washings, each holding
twenty to thirty gallons. Jesus told them, "Fill the jars
with water." So they filled them to the brim. Then he
told them, "Draw some out now and take it to the
headwaiter." So they took it. And when the headwaiter
tasted the water that had become wine, without knowing where it came from (although the servers who had
drawn the water knew), the headwaiter called the bridegroom and said to him, "Everyone serves good wine
first, and then when people have drunk freely, an infe-
rior one; but you have kept the good wine until now."

—JOHN 2:1–10

Nuptial Blessing

May almighty God bless you by the word of His mouth, and unite your hearts in the enduring bond of pure love.

May you be blessed in your children and may the love that you lavish on them be returned a hundredfold.

May the peace of Christ dwell always in your hearts and in your home; may you have true friends to stand by you, both in joy and in sorrow. May you be ready with help and consolation for all those who come to you in need; and may the blessings promised to the compassionate descend in abundance on your house.

May you be blessed in your work and enjoy its fruits. May cares never cause you distress, nor the desire for earthly possessions lead you astray; but may your hearts' concern be always for the treasures laid up for you in the life of heaven.

May the Lord grant you fullness of years, so that you may reap the harvest of a good life, and after you have served Him with loyalty in His kingdom on earth, may He take you up into His eternal dominions in Heaven.

One in Spirit

How beautiful . . . the marriage of two Christians, two who are one in hope, one in desire, one in the way of life they follow, one in the religion they practice. They are as brother and sister, both servants of the same Master. Nothing divides them, either in flesh or in spirit. They are, in very truth, two in one flesh; and where there is but one flesh there is also but one spirit. They pray together, they

worship together, they fast together; instructing one another, encouraging one another, strengthening one another. Side by side they visit God's church and partake of
God's Banquet; side by side they face difficulties and persecution, share their consolations. They have no secrets
from one another; they never shun each other's company;
they never bring sorrow to each other's hearts. Unembar-
rassed they visit the sick and assist the needy. They give
alms without anxiety; they attend the Sacrifice without
difficulty; they perform their daily exercises of piety without hindrance. They need not be furtive about making the
Sign of the Cross, nor timorous in greeting the brethren,
nor silent in asking a blessing of God. Psalms and hymns
they sing to one another, striving to see which one of them
will chant more beautifully the praises of their Lord. Hearing and seeing this, Christ rejoices. To such as these He
gives His peace. Where there are two together, there also
He is present; and where He is, there evil is not.

— TERTULLIAN (C. 160 – C. 225)

Lifelong Union

Marriage is rightly recommended to the faithful for its
fruits, the gift of children, and for the conjugal modesty of
which the mutual fidelity of the spouses is the guarantee
and bond.

But there is another reason too. In this union there is
also a mystery that makes it sacred and causes the Apostle
to say: "Husbands, love your wives as Christ has loved the
Church."

The effect of such a marriage is that man and woman once they are committed and bound to one another remain irrevocably united for their whole lives without being permitted to separate, except for the reason of adultery.

Is it not perhaps the same as with the union of Christ and his Church? They are alive together eternally; no divorce can ever separate them.

— ST. AUGUSTINE OF HIPPO (354 – 430)

Spiritual Union

"Marriage is a great sacrament: I speak in Christ and in the Church" (Ephesians 5:32). It is honorable to all, in all, and in everything, that is, in all its parts. The unmarried should esteem it in humility. It is as holy to the poor as to the rich. Its institution, its end, its purpose, its form, and its matter are all holy.

It greatly concerns the public welfare that the sanctity of marriage, which is the source of all its well-being, should be preserved inviolate.

I exhort married persons to have that mutual love that is so earnestly enjoined by the Holy Spirit in Scripture.

The first result of such love is the indissoluble union of your hearts. This spiritual union of the heart, with its affections and love, is stronger than that of mere bodily union.

The second result of this love is absolute faithfulness.

The third end of marriage is the birth and bringing up of children.

Love and faithfulness always breed confidence.

— ST. FRANCIS DE SALES (1567–1622)

Two Stubborn Pieces of Iron

Very few people ever state properly the strong argument in favor of marrying for love or against marrying for money. The argument is not that all lovers are heroes and heroines, nor is it that all dukes are profligates or all millionaires cads. The argument is this, that the differences between a man and a woman are at the best so obstinate and exasperating that they practically cannot be got over unless there is an atmosphere of exaggerated tenderness and mutual interest. To put the matter in one metaphor, the sexes are two stubborn pieces of iron; if they are to be welded together, it must be while they are red-hot. Every woman has to find out that her husband is a selfish beast, because every man is a selfish beast by the standard of a woman. But let her find out the beast while they are both still in the story of "Beauty and the Beast." Every man has to find out that his wife is cross—that is to say, sensitive to the point of madness: for every woman is mad by the masculine standard. But let him find out that she is mad while her madness is more worth considering than anyone else's sanity.

— G. K. CHESTERTON (1874–1936)

Total Surrender

Priests undergo long years of preparation in seminaries. So do all religious, male and female. But who gets preparation for marriage and where is its novitiate? Frankly, it should begin at the fathers' or mothers' knee . . . , by seeing the parents' example. . . .

The boy and girl about to marry are "in love." But do they love? Do they understand that theirs is the vocation to love—and to love so well that their children will learn love by just being their children and going into the school of their love?

Do they comprehend that love is total surrender? Do they comprehend that it is surrender to one another, for the love of God and each other? Do they understand that love never uses the pronoun *I* and is neither selfish nor self-centered? On the answer to these questions depends so much. Who can truthfully say, when they are entering marriage, that they know the answers? . . .

The two become one. The man and the woman leave parents and home and cleave to one another, becoming one flesh. This means a surrender, a giving of oneself until, in truth, two are one flesh, one mind, one heart, one soul. For those who understand this—and alas, how few they are—the veil of faith becomes gossamer thin, especially at Communion, when husband and wife become one in the heart of Christ. That is where this oneness is felt most by those who believe, and believing, see.

— CATHERINE DE HUECK DOHERTY (1900–1985)

Letter to Maria

You ask if mysticism is possible for a married woman. You say that you feel called to deep prayer but do not quite see your path, and you ask what I think.

Your question is both simple and complicated. Of course it is possible for a married person to attain to the very pinnacle of mysticism. And knowing you as I do, your deep faith, your sense of God's presence, your love for your family, your concern for the poor, I feel quite sure that you are called. You have the further advantage that David is a deeply prayerful person. It matters not that his spiritual path is a bit different from yours. Walk together. Two mystics. So, Maria, surrender to God and go on your way with confidence and joy.

Yet I do see the difficulties. The first is that most of the literature on mysticism has been written by celibates for celibates—as though mysticism was the preserve of monks and nuns. Alas, the Catholic tradition is not free from elitism. *The Cloud of Unknowing,* for example, written in fourteenth-century England, distinguishes between those called to salvation and those called to perfection. Those called to salvation are the masses of people, the laity—and for these the author will write no mystical treatise. Those called to perfection are the monks and nuns (and perhaps priests and bishops are thrown in).

The distinction between those called to salvation and those called to perfection was hit on the head by the Second Vatican Council, which declared that every Christian is called to perfection.

—— • ——

By reason of baptism every Christian is called to holiness and at times even to martyrdom; for all are called to love God with their whole heart and soul and mind and strength. The Council also spoke enthusiastically about holiness in the family, hinting at a mysticism of interpersonal relations and saying that in marriage "authentic human love is caught up into divine love."

. . . Is it by prayer in common? Or is it by uncompromising fidelity to another person? . . . You and David, together with thousands of modern people, are pioneers in the search for mysticism in family life and for a mysticism of sexuality.

One thing is clear. You will experience God as a wife and mother, just as David will experience God as a husband and father—and you both have your work. You are called to experience God in all things. . . .

Since in the mystical life one is purified by both action and suffering, remember that a great purification will take place through the struggles of married life. . . . This suffering can constitute a dark night that is no less purifying than St. John of the Cross's dark night of the soul. And it leads to an intimacy and a union and a spiritual marriage that is consummated beyond the grave.

— WILLIAM JOHNSTON (B. 1925)

The Daily Cherishing

I believe deeply that God is at work in all marriages, in the peak experiences, in the daily cherishing, in the continual reconciliation. Who can set limits to God's activity? Christians have the privilege of reflecting on this presence, of recognizing God in their marriage and pointing God out to each other, naming God by name. And over a lifetime I believe this naming changes the quality of a marriage, in an indefinable way enriching it.

At most weddings there is wine: wife and husband bring joy to each other and are glad. But Christians believe that the best wine for a wedding, the greatest gladness, comes through the transforming power of Jesus Christ. Not every couple recognizes this source of their joy, just as the steward at Cana did not know the source of the improved wine. Yet the steward had no doubt about its quality. To those who know Jesus Christ, to his disciples, he lets his glory be seen, and two-by-two they recognize him in their married love. And they believe in him.

— MARGARET GRIMER (1933 – 95)

Holy Chaos

The primeval chaos that results when I am working on a book does have its negative side beyond the lack of matching socks for six children and one husband. When this happens, it usually coincides with an influx of clothes for Poland or Mother Teresa, and Don is greeted at the door with a pile of black plastic bags that prevents him from coming into the house. Then, too, the kitchen overflows with bottles, tins, and newspapers waiting to be recycled.

When it gets to the point that the cat-food tins are all still waiting to be washed before joining the recycling pile, then tension in the house begins to rise. Then I have to stop and think again about the breadth of my vocation and find new ways of reconciling the different elements. I am reminded at such times of the advice of a Russian Orthodox Archbishop to one of his married priests who was having difficulties reconciling the demands of family life with his responsibilities as a priest. "Remember always," said the Archbishop, "that God gave you your wife before he gave you the priesthood."

— BARBARA WOOD (B. 1946)

HOLY LIVING

B^{*lessed are the poor in spirit,*}
    for theirs is the kingdom of heaven.
Blessed are they who mourn,
    for they will be comforted.
Blessed are the meek,
    for they will inherit the land.
Blessed are they who hunger and thirst for
righteousness,
    for they will be satisfied.
Blessed are the merciful,
    for they will be shown mercy.
Blessed are the clean of heart,
    for they will see God.
Blessed are the peacemakers,
    for they will be called children of God.
Blessed are they who are persecuted for the sake of
righteousness,
    for theirs is the kingdom of heaven.

—MATTHEW 5:3–10

Sing Alleluia

How happy will be our shout of Alleluia, how carefree, how secure from any adversary, where there is no enemy, where no friend perishes. There praise is offered to God, and here, too, but here it is by men who are anxious, there by men who are free from care, here by men who must die, there by men who will live forever. Here praise is offered in hope, there by men who enjoy the reality, here by men who are pilgrims on the way, there by men who have reached their own country.

So, brethren, now let us sing Alleluia, not in the enjoyment of heavenly rest, but to sweeten our toil. Sing as travelers sing along the road: but keep on walking. Solace your toil by singing—do not yield to idleness. Sing but keep on walking. What do I mean by "walking"? I mean, press on from good to better. The apostle says there are some who go from bad to worse. But if you press on, you keep on walking. Go forward then in virtue, in true faith and right conduct. Sing up—and keep on walking.

— ST. AUGUSTINE OF HIPPO (354 – 430)

Prayer of St. Francis

Lord, make me an instrument of your peace.
Where there is hatred, let me sow love.
Where there is injury, pardon.
Where there is doubt, faith.
Where there is despair, hope.
Where there is darkness, light.
Where there is sadness, joy.

O Divine Master, grant that I may not so much seek
to be consoled, as to console;
to be understood, as to understand;
to be loved, as to love;
for it is in giving that we receive,
it is in pardoning that we are pardoned,
it is in dying that we are born to eternal life.

— ATTRIBUTED TO ST. FRANCIS OF ASSISI
(C. 1181–1226)

St. Francis of Assisi's True Joy

Blessed Francis called Brother Leo and said: "Brother Leo,
write." He responded: "Look, I'm ready!" "Write," he said,
"what true joy is."

"A messenger arrives and says that all the Masters of
Paris have entered the Order. Write: this isn't true joy! Or,
that all the prelates, archbishops, and bishops beyond the
mountains, as well as the King of France and the King of
England [have entered the Order]. Write: this isn't true joy!
Again, that my brothers have gone to the nonbelievers and
converted all of them to the faith; again, that I have so
much grace from God that I heal the sick and perform
many miracles. I tell you true joy doesn't consist in any of
these things."

———— • ————

"Then what is true joy?"

"I return from Perugia and arrive here in the dead of
night. It's wintertime, muddy and so cold that icicles have
formed on the edges of my habit and keep striking my legs

and blood flows from such wounds. Freezing, covered with mud and ice, I come to the gate, and after I've knocked and called for some time, a brother comes and asks: 'Who are you?' 'Brother Francis,' I answer. 'Go away!' he says. 'This is not a decent hour to be wandering about! You may not come in!' When I insist, he replies: 'Go away! You are simple and stupid! Don't come back to us again! There are many of us here like you—we don't need you!' I stand again at the door and say: 'For the love of God, take me in tonight!' And he replies: 'I will not! Go to the Crosiers's place and ask there!'

"I tell you this: If I had patience and did not become upset, true joy, as well as true virtue and the salvation of my soul, would consist in this."
(St. Francis of Assisi: c. 1181–1226)

Look for Jesus

In life and in death keep close to Jesus and give yourself into his faithful keeping; he alone can help you when all others fail you. He is of such a kind, this beloved friend of yours, that he will not share your love with another; he wishes to have your heart for himself alone, to reign there like a king seated on his rightful throne. If only you knew the way to empty your heart of all things created! If you did, how gladly would Jesus come and make his home with you! When you put your trust in men, excluding Jesus, you will find that it is nearly all a complete loss. Have no faith in a reed that shakes in the wind, don't try leaning upon it; mortal things are but grass, remember, the glory of them is but grass in flower and will fall. Look only

at a man's outward guise and you will quickly be led astray;
look to others to console you and bring you benefit, and
as often as not you will find you have suffered loss. If you
look for Jesus in everything, you will certainly find him;
but if it's yourself you're looking for, it's yourself you're
going to find, and that to your own hurt, because a man is
a greater bane to himself, if he doesn't look for Jesus, than
the whole world is, or the whole host of his enemies.

— THOMAS À KEMPIS (C. 1380–1471)

Lead, Kindly Light

Lead, kindly Light, amid the encircling gloom,
Lead thou me on;
The night is dark, and I am far from home,
Lead thou me on.
Keep thou my feet; I do not ask to see
The distant scene; one step enough for me.

I was not ever thus, nor prayed that thou
Shouldst lead me on;
I loved to choose and see my path; but now
Lead thou me on.
I loved the garish day, and, spite of fears,
Pride ruled my will: remember not past years.

So long thy power hath blest me, sure it still
Will lead me on
O'er moor and fen, o'er crag and torrent, till
The night is gone,

And with the morn those Angel faces smile,
Which I have loved long since, and lost awhile.

— VENERABLE JOHN HENRY NEWMAN
(1801–90)

The Helping Hand of Caroline Chisholm

Mrs. Chisholm is a lady who is not rich, or related to any great people; but she has been engaged nearly all her life in helping laboring and poor people, by teaching them how to help themselves; and she has succeeded so well, that there are thousands who look upon her with feelings of as much affection as if she were their mother. . . .

She has a husband, who has gone out to Australia lately to help her good work, and six children; from morning until late at night any man or woman, or young girl, no matter how humble, how poorly dressed, is welcome to come and consult her, and tell her their griefs. At breakfast, dinner, tea, and supper, she is at the command of the unhappy and distressed; and when she is not talking, she is writing letters. For besides all those in England who consult her, hundreds and hundreds of people in Australia send to her to get their relations out to join them. Mrs. Chisholm never asks what country or what religion anyone is who comes to her; but she just sets about to see the way of helping them to get out of their difficulties. (*Caroline Chisholm: 1808–77*)

— TRELAWNEY SAUNDERS

Hard to Love

We are not expecting utopia here on this earth. But God meant things to be much easier than we have made them. A man has a natural right to food, clothing, and shelter. A certain amount of goods is necessary to lead a good life. A family needs work as well as bread. Property is proper to man. We must keep repeating these things. Eternal life begins now. "All the way to heaven is heaven, because He said, 'I am the Way.'" The Cross is there of course, but "in the Cross is joy of spirit." And love makes all things easy. If we are putting off the old man and putting on Christ, then we are walking in love, and love is all that we want. But it is hard to love, from the human standpoint and from the divine standpoint, in a two-room apartment.

— DOROTHY DAY (1897–1980)

Venerable Margaret Sinclair

Margaret's sense of humor never left her, even when facing death. One is reminded of her fellow countryman, St. John Ogilvie, Jesuit and martyr. When he was on his way to the scaffold in Glasgow in 1615, a Presbyterian minister, shocked at the apparent levity with which he was laughing with those around him, asked if he were not afraid to be so merry when he was so near his death. "We have a proverb in Scotland," replied the priest: "It's past joking when the head's off!"

"One day," says one of the Sisters, "when Margaret was still able to be up for a little while with the other invalids, a new nun, by name Sister Clare, was brought in.

Margaret glanced at her. 'She is the only lady among you,' she said calmly to the others. They were slightly aston- ished. 'You are all Sister Bernard or Sister John or Sister Columba,' she explained, laughing."
(Venerable Margaret Sinclair: 1900–25)

— F. A. FORBES

True Happiness

Do you want to know the secret of true happiness? Of deep and genuine peace? Do you want to solve at a blow all your difficulties in relations with your neighbor, bring all polemic to an end, avoid all dissension?

Well, decide here and now to love things and men as Jesus loved them, that is, to the point of self-sacrifice. Do not bother with the bookkeeping of love; love without keeping accounts.

If you know someone who is decent and likable, love him, but if someone else is very unlikable, love him just the same. If someone greets you and smiles, greet him and smile back, but if someone else treads on your feet, smile just the same. If someone does you a good turn, thank the Lord for it, but if someone else slanders you, persecutes you, curses you, strikes you, thank him and carry on.

Do not say: "I'm right, he's wrong." Say: "I must love him as myself." This is the kind of love Jesus taught: a love that transforms, vivifies, enriches, brings peace.

— CARLO CARRETTO (1910–88)

Call within a Call

At the beginning, between twelve and eighteen, I didn't want to become a nun. We were a very happy family. But when I was eighteen, I decided to leave my home and become a nun. I wanted to be a missionary, I wanted to go out and give the life of Christ to the people in the missionary countries. At that time some missionaries had gone to India from Yugoslavia. They told me the Loreto nuns were doing work in Calcutta and other places. I offered myself to go out to the Bengal Mission, and they sent me to India in 1929.

I took the first vows in Loreto in 1931. Then in 1937 I took final vows in Loreto. At Loreto I was in charge of a school in the Bengali department. At that time many of the girls that are now with me were girls in school. I was teaching them.

In 1946 I was going to Darjeeling, to make my retreat. It was in that train, I heard the call to give up all and follow Jesus into the slums to serve Him among the poorest of the poor. I knew it was His will, and that I had to follow Him. There was no doubt that it was going to be His work.

— MOTHER TERESA OF CALCUTTA (1910 – 97)

TRANSFORMING THE LIFE: GROWTH AND SERVICE

"Follow me," said Jesus. Christian history is, in large part, the story of Christians wrestling with what this means. In following Jesus, Christians have looked to the lives of the Lord's disciples for inspiration. Jesus' disciples shared his way of life and were sustained by his teaching and example. The disciples were also united with Jesus through their suffering, and they died with the hope of one day being resurrected, as Jesus was.

Christian tradition understands discipleship as something deeper than simply following Jesus. It involves "imitation of Christ"—striving to conform oneself to Jesus in as many respects as possible. The disciple can hope to do this successfully because Christ lives in his followers. As Paul said, "I have been crucified with Christ; yet I live, no longer I, but Christ lives in me" (Gal. 2:19–20).

MINISTRY

Then Jesus approached and said to them, "All power in heaven and on earth has been given to me. Go, therefore, and make disciples of all nations, baptizing them in the name of the Father, and of the Son, and of the holy Spirit, teaching them to observe all that I have commanded you. And behold, I am with you always, until the end of the age."

—MATTHEW 28:18–20

Send the Remedy

Godhead,
my love,
I have one thing to ask of you.
When the world was lying sick
you sent your only-begotten Son as doctor,
and I know you did it for love.
But now I see the world lying completely dead—
so dead that my soul faints at the sight.
What way can there be now
to revive this dead one once more?
For you, God, cannot suffer,

and you are not about to come again
to redeem the world but to judge it.
How then
shall this dead one be brought back to life?
I do not believe, O infinite goodness,
that you have no remedy.
Indeed, I proclaim it:
your love is not wanting,
nor is your power weakened,
nor is your wisdom lessened.
So you want to, you can,
and you know how to
send the remedy that is needed.
I beg you then,
let it please your goodness
to show me the remedy,
and let my soul be roused to pick it up courageously.

— ST. CATHERINE OF SIENA (C.1347– 80)

Spiritual Mothers

Mothers of families, even if they had a thousand sons and daughters, would still find room for every single one in their hearts, because that is how true love works. It even seems that the more children a mother has, the greater is her love and care for each one individually. With still more reason spiritual mothers can and should so act, since spiritual love is beyond comparison more powerful than human love.

Therefore, dearest mothers, if you love these dear children of yours with true and selfless charity, it will be impossible for you not to have them all clearly present in your memory and in your heart.

I ask you, please, do try to bring them up with love, with a gentle and kindly hand, not overbearingly nor harshly. Try to be kind always. Notice what Jesus Christ says, "Learn of me for I am gentle and humble of heart." And of God we read, "He orders all things graciously." That is, he arranges and governs all things gently. And again Jesus Christ says, "My yoke, my service, is light and sweet."

That is how you yourselves must try to act, using all possible gentleness. And above all, be careful not to use force, because God has given free will to everybody and wants to force nobody, but only points out, invites, and counsels. I do not mean, however, that at times one must not make use of some restraint, even of severity in some cases, depending on the importance of the circumstances and the need of the individuals. But even then, we must be moved solely by charity and zeal for souls.

— ST. ANGELA MERICI (1474–1540)

From Village to Village

We went through the villages of the new converts who received baptism a few years ago. No Portuguese lives in these parts [of India], which are utterly barren and poverty-stricken. The native Christians are without any priest. The only thing they know about Christianity is that they are Christians. There is no one to offer Mass for them; no one to teach them the Creed, the Our Father, the Hail Mary, the commandments.

So, since I came here, I have had no rest. I have been going from village to village and every child not yet baptized I have baptized. So I have brought redemption to a very great number of children who, as the saying goes, cannot tell their right hand from their left. But the children would not let me say my office or eat or rest till I had taught them some prayer. It was then that I really began to feel that of such is the kingdom of heaven.

I could not reject so religious a request without myself being irreligious. I made a start with the sign of the cross, and taught them the Apostles' Creed, the Our Father, and the Hail Mary. I saw immediately that they were very intelligent. If only there were someone to train them in the principles of Christianity, I am sure that they would be extremely good Christians.

— ST. FRANCIS XAVIER (1506 – 52)

More Learning Than Love

Very many out here fail to become Christians simply because there is nobody available to make them Christian. I have very often had the notion to go around the universities of Europe, and especially Paris, and to shout aloud everywhere like a madman, and to bludgeon those people who have more learning than love, with these words, "Alas, what an immense number of souls are excluded from heaven through your fault and thrust down to hell!"

If only those people devoted themselves to this care in the way they do to literature. Then they would be able to render God an account of their doctrine and of the talents entrusted to them!

Many of them, moved by this thought, and helped by meditation on the things of God, would take pains to hear what the Lord is speaking in them and, putting aside their own selfish desires and worldly matters, would put themselves fully at God's beck and call. They would indeed cry from their soul: "Lord, here I am. What would you have me do? Send me wherever you wish, even as far as India."

— ST. FRANCIS XAVIER (1506 – 52)

Freedom to Captives

Yesterday, 30 May 1627, the feast of the Most Holy Trinity, a great number of black people who had been seized from along the African rivers were put ashore [in Colombia] from one very large vessel. We hurried out with two baskets full of oranges, lemons, sweet biscuits, and all sorts of other things. When we reached their huts it was like entering another Guinea. We had to force our way through the crowds till we reached the sick. There was a great number of them, lying on the damp earth, or rather in mud; but someone had formed the idea of making a heap of tiles and broken bricks in case the damp should be too much for them. This was all they had for a bed, all the more uncomfortable because they were naked without any covering at all.

We took off our cloaks, went to a store, brought from there all the wood that was available, and put it together to make a platform; then, forcing a way through the guards, we eventually managed to carry all the sick onto it. Then we separated them into two groups; one of them my companion addressed with the aid of an interpreter, the other I spoke to myself.

Two of the black slaves were more dead than alive; they were already cold, and we could hardly feel any pulse in their veins. We got together some glowing embers on a tile, placed the dying men near them, and then threw aromatic spices on the fire. We had two bags of these spices, and used them all. Then with the help of our cloaks—for the slaves have none of their own, and it would have been a waste of time to ask their masters—we got them to inhale the vapors, which seemed to restore their warmth and vitality. You should have seen the expression of gratitude in their eyes!

—— • ——

In this way we spoke to them, not with words but with deeds; and for people in their situation who were convinced that they had been brought there to be eaten, any other form of address would have been pointless. Then we sat or knelt beside them and washed their faces and bodies with wine; by such acts of kindness we tried to cheer them up, and performed for them all the natural services that are calculated to raise the spirits of the sick.

Then we began to instruct them for baptism. We first explained to them the wonderful effects of the sacrament on both body and soul, and when they showed by their answers to our questions that they understood us sufficiently well, we began to teach them at greater length concerning the one God who rewards and punishes each according to his deserts, and so on. We urged them to repent and give some indication of sorrow for their sins. Finally, when they seemed to be sufficiently prepared, we explained to them the mysteries of the Trinity, Incarnation, and Passion. We showed them a representation of Christ crucified above a baptismal font, into which the blood flowed from his wounds. Then we taught them to repeat after us the act of contrition in their own language.

— ST. PETER CLAVER (1581–1654)

Children Evangelize Children

Nano Nagle of Cork was well aware of the status God gave to the poor. What was done to the least of them was done to Him. Each one of them was made in the image of God and made out of love. Personal dignity, personal worth, depended on that love. This was the essence of religion and the essence of Nano's educational system. Her pupils were not only well instructed in the faith but were so brought up to love instructing others. Herein was the secret of her success; her pupils were convinced that they had good news to tell.

"All my children are brought up to be fond of instructing, as I think it lies in the power of the poor to be of more service that way than the rich."

A notable point about Nano was that she addressed herself to those who could not read at all. For an illiterate people, the spoken word was very important.

She elicited a promise from those emigrating from Ireland to the West Indies that they "would take great pains with the little blacks to instruct them." Pictures were at once visual aids and little gifts for the native West Indians, miniatures of the Good News and ready access to the gospel story. The Irish victims of injustice brought the

good news of Jesus Christ to those more abject still. Children evangelized children.
(*Nano Nagle: c. 1718–84*)

Constant Prayer

St. Jean-Baptiste Vianney was sure that "a good priest must be devoted to constant prayer. . . .

"The thing that keeps us priests from gaining sanctity is thoughtlessness. It annoys us to turn our minds away from external affairs; we do not know what we really ought to do. What we need is deep reflection, together with prayer and an intimate union with God.

"We are beggars who must ask God for everything. . . . How many people we can call back to God by our prayers." And he used to say over and over again: "Ardent prayer addressed to God: this is our greatest happiness on earth."

And he enjoyed this happiness abundantly when his mind rose with the help of heavenly light to contemplate the things of heaven, and his pure and simple soul rose with all its deepest love from the mystery of the incarnation to the Heights of the Holy Trinity. The crowds of pilgrims who surrounded him in the church could feel something coming forth from the depths of the inner life of this humble priest when words like these burst forth from his inflamed breast, as they often did: "To be loved by God, to be joined to God, to walk before God, to live for God, O blessed life, O blessed death."
(*St. Jean-Baptiste Vianney: 1786–1859*)

— POPE JOHN XXIII (1881–1963)

A True Father

If we want to be thought of as men who have the real happiness of our pupils at heart and who help each to fulfill his role in life, you must never forget that you are taking the place of parents who love their children. I have always worked, studied, and exercised my priesthood out of love for them. And not I alone, but the whole Salesian Order.

My sons, how often in my long career has this great truth come home to me! It is so much easier to get angry than to be patient, to threaten a boy rather than persuade him. I would even say that usually it is so much more convenient for our own impatience and pride to punish them than to correct them patiently with firmness and gentleness.

I recommend to you the love St. Paul had for his new converts. When he found them inattentive and unresponsive to his love, that same love led him to tears and prayers.

Be careful not to give anyone reason to think that you act under the impulse of anger. It is difficult to keep calm when administering punishment. But it is very necessary if you are not to give the impression that you are simply asserting your authority or giving vent to your anger.

—— • ——

Let us look on those over whom we have a certain authority, as sons. Let us be determined to be at their service, even as Jesus came to obey, and not to command. We should be ashamed to give the least impression of domineering. We should only exercise authority in order the better to serve the boys.

That was how Jesus treated his apostles. He put up with their ignorance and dullness and their lack of faith.

His attitude toward sinners was full of kindness and loving friendship. This astonished some and scandalized others, but to others it gave enough hope to ask forgiveness from God.

Because the boys are our sons, we must put aside all anger when we correct their faults, or at least restrain it so much that it is almost completely suppressed. There must be no angry outburst, no look of contempt, no hurtful words. Instead, like true fathers, really intent on their correction and improvement, show them compassion at the present moment and hold out hope for the future.

In serious matters it is better to ask God's help in humble prayer, than to make a long speech that wounds those who hear it and does no good at all to the guilty ones.

— ST. JOHN BOSCO (1815 – 88)

St. Anthony's Pigs

Here [New Orleans] I have invented a way to collect a little more money to enlarge the orphanage. I took the money box shaped like a little pig, which they call St. Anthony's pigs here, and the people compete to see who is able to fatten it, that is, fill it up with nickels. In three days the sisters gave out 150 and I want them to give out a thousand. There are various sizes, the smallest, which we give to the more trustworthy schoolchildren, can hold $5, others $10, others $20. Can you imagine what a fine collection? You should do the same thing right away, and if you don't find the pig, take another form, but do it immediately for the month of St. Anthony. For the close of the

month the money boxes will all be full at the altar of the
saint. . . . Set your wits to work!

— ST. FRANCES XAVIER CABRINI (1850–1917)

The Legion of Mary

Confer, O Lord, on us,
Who serve beneath the standard of Mary,
That fullness of faith in you and trust in her,
To which it is given to conquer the world.
Grant us a lively faith, animated by charity,
Which will enable us to perform all our actions
From the motive of pure love of you,
And ever to see you and serve you in our neighbor;
A faith, firm and immovable as a rock,
Through which we shall rest tranquil and steadfast
Amid the crosses, toils, and disappointments of life;
A courageous faith that will inspire us
To undertake and carry out without hesitation
Great things for your glory and for the salvation of souls;
A faith that will be our Legion's Pillar of Fire—
To lead us forth united—
To kindle everywhere the fires of divine love—
To enlighten those who are in darkness and in the
    shadow of death—
To inflame those who are lukewarm—
To bring back life to those who are dead in sin;
And that will guide our own feet in the way of peace;
So that—the battle of life over—
Our Legion may reassemble,

Without the loss of anyone,
In the kingdom of your love and glory.

— FRANK DUFF (1889–1980)

Unworthy Poor

God is on the side even of the unworthy poor, as we know from the story Jesus told of His Father and the prodigal son. Readers may object that the prodigal son returned penitent to his father's house. But who knows, he might have gone out and squandered money on the next Saturday night; he might have refused to help with the farmwork, and asked to be sent to finish his education instead, thereby further incurring his brother's righteous wrath, and the war between the worker and the intellectual, or the conservative and the radical, would be on. Jesus has another answer to that one: to forgive one's brother seventy times seven. There are always answers, although they are not always calculated to soothe.

— DOROTHY DAY (1897–1980)

The Face of Jesus

Today I baptized thirty adults and children. And not only from here; for the Christians make their way through the mountains from Miyahara, Kuzushima, and Haratsuka. I then heard more than fifty confessions. After Sunday Mass for the first time I intoned and recited the prayers in Japanese with the people. The peasants stare at me, their eyes alive with curiosity. And as I speak there often arises in my mind the face of one who preached the Sermon on the Mount; and I imagine the people who sat or knelt fascinated by his words. As for me, perhaps I am so fascinated by his face because the Scriptures make no mention of it. Precisely because it is not mentioned, all its details are left to my imagination. From childhood I have clasped that face to my breast just like the person who romantically idealizes the countenance of one he loves. While I was still a student, studying in the seminary, if ever I had a sleepless night, his beautiful face would rise up in my heart.

— SHUSAKU ENDO (1923 – 96)

SPIRITUAL GUIDANCE

Peter turned and saw the disciple following whom Jesus loved, the one who had also reclined upon his chest during the supper and had said, "Master, who is the one who will betray you?" When Peter saw him, he said to Jesus, "Lord, what about him?" Jesus said to him, "What if I want him to remain until I come? What concern is it of yours? You follow me."

—JOHN 21:20–22

Old and New

First drink from the Old Testament, so that you may drink from the New as well. You cannot drink from the second without drinking from the first. Drink from the Old Testament to slake your thirst, and from the New to quench it completely. Compunction is found in the Old Testament, joy in the New.

Drink Christ because he is the vine; drink Christ because he is the rock that poured out water. Drink Christ because he is the fountain of life; drink Christ because he is the river whose running waters give joy to the city of God, and because he is peace, and because out of his heart will flow rivers of living water. Drink Christ to drink the blood that redeemed you; drink Christ to drink his words: The Old Testament is his word; the New Testament is his word. Holy scripture is drunk and swallowed when the power of the eternal Word penetrates the depths of the mind and the virtue of the soul. In short, we do not live by bread alone, but by every word of God. Drink this word, but according to its own order. Drink it first in the Old Testament; then hasten to drink it also in the New.

— ST. AMBROSE OF MILAN (C. 339 – 97)

Wise Leadership

As often as any important business has to be done in the monastery, let the abbot call together the whole community and himself set forth the matter. And, having heard the advice of the brethren, let him take counsel with himself and then do what he shall judge to be most expedient. Now the reason why we have said that all should be called to council, is that God often reveals what is better to the younger. Let the brethren give their advice with all deference and humility, nor venture to defend their opinions obstinately; but let the decision depend rather on the abbot's judgment, so that when he has decided what is the better course, all may obey. However, just as it is proper for disciples to obey their master, so is it becoming that he on his part should dispose all things with prudence and justice.

— • —

Let [the abbot] study rather to be loved than feared. Let him not be turbulent or anxious, overbearing or obstinate, jealous or too suspicious, for otherwise he will never be at rest. Let him be prudent and considerate in all his commands; and whether the work that he enjoins concern God or the world, let him always be discreet and moderate, bearing in mind the discretion of holy Jacob, who said: If I cause my flocks to be overdriven, they will all perish in one day. So, imitating these and other examples of discretion, the mother of the virtues, let him so temper all things that the strong may still have something to long after, and the weak may not draw back in alarm. And, especially, let him keep this present Rule in all things; so that having ministered faithfully, he may hear from the Lord what the good servant heard who gave his fellow servants wheat in due season: Amen, I say unto you, he will set him over all his goods.

— ST. BENEDICT OF NURSIA (C. 480 – C. 547)

Love the Lord

Be compassionate toward the poor, the destitute, and the afflicted; and, as far as lies in your power, help and console them. Give thanks to God for all the gifts he has bestowed upon you, so that you will become worthy of still greater gifts. Toward your subjects, act with such justice that you may steer a middle course, swerving neither to the right nor to the left, but lean more to the side of the poor man than of the rich until such time as you are certain about the truth. Do your utmost to ensure peace and justice for all your subjects but especially for clergy and religious.

Devotedly obey our mother, the Roman Church, and revere the Supreme Pontiff as your spiritual father. Endeavor to banish all sin, especially blasphemy and heresy, from your kingdom.

Finally, my dear son, I impart to you every blessing that a loving father can bestow on his son; may the Father, Son, and Holy Spirit, and all the saints, guard you from all evil. May the Lord grant you the grace to do his will so that he may be served and honored by you, and that, together, after this life we may come to see him, love him, and praise him forever.

—St. Louis IX (1214–70)

The Hidden God

If you want to be without sin and perfect, don't chatter about God. Nor should you (seek to) understand anything about God, for God is above all understanding. One master says: "If I had a God I could understand, I would no longer consider him God." So, if you understand anything of Him, that is not He, and by understanding anything of Him you fall into misunderstanding, and from this misunderstanding you fall into brutishness, for whatever in creatures is uncomprehending is brutish. So, if you don't want to become brutish, understand nothing of God the unutterable.

———•———

Indeed, if a man thinks he will get more of God by meditation, by devotion, by ecstasies, or by special infusion of grace than by the fireside or in the stable, that is nothing but taking God, wrapping a cloak around His head, and shoving Him under a bench. For whoever seeks God in a special way gets the way and misses God, who lies hidden in it. But whoever seeks God without any special way gets Him as He is in Himself, and that man lives with the Son, and He is life itself.

— MEISTER ECKHART (C. 1260 – C. 1328)

True Guidance

Those who guide souls should realize that the principal agent and guide and motive force in this matter is not them *but the Holy Spirit, who never fails in his care* for people; they are only instruments to guide people to perfection by faith and the law of God, according to the spirit *that God is giving* to the individual person.

— ST. JOHN OF THE CROSS (1542 – 91)

Dryness in Prayer

There are three tests to ascertain whether dryness in prayer is the result of God's purgation or of our own sins.

The first is when we find no comfort either in the things of God or in created things. For when God brings the soul into the dark night in order to wean it from sweetness and to purify its sensual desires, he does not allow it to find sweetness or comfort anywhere.

The second is that the memory is ordinarily centered on God with painful anxiety and carefulness. The spirit becomes strong, more vigilant, and more careful lest there be any negligence in serving God.

The third sign is inability to meditate or make reflections, and to excite the imagination as before, despite all the efforts we may make. For God now begins to communicate himself, no longer through the channels of sense as formerly, but in pure spirit.

— ST. JOHN OF THE CROSS (1542 – 91)

The Finished Product

All goes well when God is, so to speak, both the author and the object of our faith, the one complementing and augmenting the other. It is like the right side of a beautiful tapestry being worked stitch by stitch on the reverse side. Neither the stitches nor the needle are visible, but, one by one, those stitches make a magnificent pattern that only becomes apparent when the work is completed and the right side exposed to the light of day; although while it is in progress there is no sign of its beauty and wonder.

The same applies to self-surrendered souls who see only God and their duty. The accomplishment of that duty is at each moment one imperceptible stitch added to the tapestry. And yet it is with these stitches that God performs wonders of which one occasionally has a presentiment at the time, but which will not be fully known until the great day of judgment.

— JEAN-PIERRE DE CAUSSADE (1675 –1751)

Daily Duty

Let not a day pass without employing at least one quarter of an hour in reading some spiritual book; and a more considerable time on Sundays and holidays; advise with your director what books may be most proper, and endeavor to procure them for yourself and your family. . . . As you are praying, you are speaking to God, so when you are reading or hearing his word, he is speaking to you. As then you desire he should hear you when you speak to him; so take you care to hearken faithfully to him when he speaks to you.

— RICHARD CHALLONER (1691–1781)

Pray as You Can

Prayer, in the sense of union with God, is the most crucifying thing there is. One must do it for God's sake; but one will not get any satisfaction out of it, in the sense of feeling "I am good at prayer," "I have an infallible method." That would be disastrous, since what we want to learn is precisely our own weakness, powerlessness, unworthiness. Nor ought one to expect "a sense of the reality of the supernatural" of which you speak. And one should wish for no prayer, except precisely the prayer that God gives us— probably very distracted and unsatisfactory in every way!

On the other hand, the only way to pray is to pray; and the way to pray well is to pray much. If one has no time for this, then one must at least pray regularly. But the less one prays, the worse it goes. And if circumstances do not permit even regularity, then one must put up with the fact that when one does try to pray, one can't pray—and our prayer will probably consist of telling this to God.

— • —

The rule is simply: *Pray as you can, and do not try to pray as you can't.*

Take yourself as you find yourself, and start from that.

—JOHN CHAPMAN (1865–1933)

Trust in God

When the soul grieves and is afraid of offending God, it does not offend Him and is very far from committing sin. Divine grace is with you continually and you are very dear to the Lord. Shadows and fears and convictions to the contrary are diabolical stratagems that you should despise in the name of Jesus. Do not listen to these temptations. The spirit of evil is busily engaged in trying to make you believe that your past life has been all strewn with sins.

Listen, rather, to me when I tell you, just as we are told by the Spouse of our souls, that your present state is an effect of your love for God and a proof of his incomparable love for you. Cast away those fears, dispel those shadows that the devil is increasing in your soul in order to torment you and drive you away, if possible, even from daily Communion. . . .

Never fall back on yourself alone, but place all your trust in God and don't be too eager to be set free from your present state. Let the Holy Spirit act within you. Give yourself up to all his transports and have no fear. He is so wise and gentle and discreet that He never brings about anything but good. How good this Holy Spirit, this Comforter, is to all, but how supremely good He is to those who seek Him!

— BLESSED PADRE PIO (1887–1968)

Into Thy Hands

Lately I learned something that made me understand as never before the beauty of the habit of prayer. A Jew was telling me that he so wished in these days [during the 1939–45 war] that he had faith; he was building a sandbag wall and foolishly I had dropped my crucifix into it; he insisted on undoing his wall and getting it for me. He was a stranger, and I did not know him; he was standing holding my crucifix, looking at it with a puzzled wistfulness. "Of course," he said, "I'm a Jew, my mother was a good Jewess, I never learned nothing about Christ, we don't bother to, but I did learn to say my prayers day and night, and I wish I 'ad kept it up."

"What did you say?" I asked.

"Well, the morning ones was long, but the night was short; all us little Jew kids said it as we fell asleep."

"What was it?"

"Well, Miss, it went like this: 'Father, into Thy hands I commend my spirit.' It's what mothers teached little Jewish boys ever since the world began, they do say. They tells 'em to say it just before they falls asleep."

— CARYLL HOUSELANDER (1901–54)

God Gives Us Everything

Prayer is the most difficult thing in the world for human beings. To pray is to remain face-to-face with the Invisible. Prayer is said to be the lifting of the soul to God. That is very hard for us because we need sensible and visible objects; hence we are always on the lookout for pretexts to diminish the place of prayer in our life.

—•—

The subject matter of prayer is of little importance; what matters above all is the degree of our love. We must realize that if, in terms of love, God gives us everything, he often gives us little in terms of light. The domain of knowledge here below is always limited; only in heaven, in the beatific vision, will knowledge be complete.

—•—

We must always let the Holy Spirit do as he pleases with us. Nevertheless, seeing how important Mary is, we have the right to ask our Lord—if we have understood these things—to give us a deeper understanding of this mystery, to lead us into that intimacy with Mary that he himself had, and to let us experience a little of the trust he had in her.

— THOMAS PHILIPPE (1905 – 93)

A Burden to Others

In order to face suffering in peace: suffer without imposing on others a theory of suffering, . . . without proclaiming yourself a martyr, without counting out the price of your courage, without disdaining sympathy, and without seeking too much of it.

We must be sincere in our sufferings as in anything else. We must recognize at once our weakness and our pain, but we do not need to advertise them. We must face the fact that it is much harder to stand the long monotony of slight suffering than a passing onslaught of intense pain.

In either case, what is hard is our own poverty, and the spectacle of our own selves reduced more and more to nothing, wasting away in our own estimation and in that of our friends. We must be willing to accept also the bitter truth that, in the end, we may have to become a burden to those who love us.

But it is necessary that we face this also. It takes heroic charity and humility to let others sustain us when we are absolutely incapable of sustaining ourselves.

We cannot suffer well unless we see Christ everywhere—both in suffering and in the charity of those who come to the aid of our affliction.

— THOMAS MERTON (1915 – 68)

SPIRITUAL FRIENDSHIP

No one has greater love than this, to lay down one's life for one's friends. You are my friends if you do what I command you. I no longer call you slaves, because a slave does not know what his master is doing. I have called you friends, because I have told you everything I have heard from my Father. It was not you who chose me, but I who chose you and appointed you to go and bear fruit that will remain, so that whatever you ask the Father in my name he may give you.

—JOHN 15:13–16

My Friend Basil

Not only did I myself hold my friend, the great Basil, in high regard for his seriousness of character and the maturity and prudence of his discourse, but I also persuaded other young men who did not know him to share my sentiments. For he was already respected by many of them since his renown had preceded him. . . .

We seemed to have a single soul animating two bodies. And, while those who claim that all things are in all things are not readily to be believed, we, at least, had to believe that we were in and with each other.

The sole ambition of both of us was virtue and a life so led in view of future hopes, as to sever our attachment to this life before we had to depart it.

With this in view we directed our life and actions, following the guidance of the divine precept, and at the same time spurring each other to virtue. And, if it is not too much to say it, we were for each other a rule and a scales for the discernment of good and evil.

Different men have different names, derived from their ancestors or their own pursuits and deeds. Our great concern, our great name, was to be Christians and be called Christians.

— ST. GREGORY OF NAZIANZUS (C. 329 – 90)

St. Scholastica and St. Benedict

St. Benedict's sister, Scholastica, who had been consecrated to almighty God in early childhood, used to visit her brother once a year. On these occasions he would go down to meet her in a house belonging to the monastery, a short distance from the entrance.

For this particular visit he joined her there with a few of his disciples and they spent the whole day singing God's praises and conversing about the spiritual life. When darkness was setting in, they took their meal together and continued their conversation at table until it was quite late. Then the holy nun said to him, "Please do not leave me tonight; let us keep on talking about the joys of heaven till morning."

"What are you saying, sister?" he replied. "You know I cannot stay away from the monastery."

At her brother's refusal, Scholastica folded her hands on the table and rested her head upon them in earnest prayer. When she looked up again, there was a sudden burst of lightning and thunder, accompanied by such a downpour that Benedict and his companions were unable to set foot outside the door.

— • —

Realizing that he could not return to the monastery in this terrible storm, Benedict complained bitterly. "God forgive you, sister," he said. "What have you done?"

Scholastica simply answered, "When I appealed to you, you would not listen to me. So I turned to my God and he heard my prayer. Leave now if you can. Leave me here and go back to your monastery."

This, of course, he could not do. He had no choice now but to stay, in spite of his unwillingness. They spent the entire night together and both of them derived great profit from the holy converse they had about the interior life.

We need not be surprised that in this instance the woman proved mightier than her brother. Do we not read in St. John that God is love? Surely it is no more than right that her influence was greater than his, since hers was the greater love.

Three days later as he stood in his room looking up toward the sky, the man of God beheld his sister's soul leaving her body and entering the court of heaven in the form of a dove.

Overjoyed at her eternal glory, he gave thanks to almighty God in hymns of praise. Then, he sent some of his

brethren to bring her body to the monastery and bury it in the tomb he had prepared for himself. The bodies of these two were now to share a common resting place just as in life their souls had always been one in God.
(St. Scholastica: c. 480–543)

— ST. GREGORY THE GREAT (C. 540 – 604)

To Dom Gondulph

Whenever I make up my mind to write to you, soul most beloved of my soul, whenever I make up my mind to write, I feel puzzled to know how best to begin. My feeling toward you is indeed sweetness and song to my heart, and I wish you the greatest blessings my mind can devise. From the moment I laid eyes on you, you know how deeply I loved you; I hear reports of you that make me long after you, God alone knows to what extent; and so wherever you wander my affection follows you, and wherever I remain, my desire encircles you. But when you beg me by your messengers, urge me by your letters, importune me by your gifts to keep you in remembrance, then let my tongue stick fast to the roof of my mouth if I remember thee not (Psalm 136:6), if I find in anyone but Gondulph the very perfection of friendship. How should I ever forget you? How could he perish from memory who is impressed upon my heart as a seal on wax?

Now tell me: why do you complain with such a mournful face that you never receive a line from me? Why do you ask with such affection that I should write frequently, when you have me always with you in thought?

When you keep silence, I realize that you love me; and when I make no sign, surely thou knowest that I love thee (John 21:16)? You are constantly present in my mind because I never for a moment doubt you, and I hereby swear to you that you can feel equally certain of me.

— ST. ANSELM OF CANTERBURY (C. 1033–1109)

The Best Medicine

What happiness, what security, what joy to have someone to whom you dare to speak on terms of equality as to another self; one to whom you need have no fear to confess your failings; one to whom you can unblushingly make known what progress you have made in the spiritual life; one to whom you can entrust all the secrets of your heart and before whom you can place all your plans! What, therefore, is more pleasant than so to unite to oneself the spirit of another and of two to form one, that no boasting is thereafter to be feared, no suspicion to be dreaded, no correction of one by the other to cause pain, no praise on the part of one to bring a charge of adulation from the other. "A friend," says the Wise Man, "is the medicine of life." Excellent, indeed, is that saying. For medicine is not more powerful or more efficacious for our wounds in all our temporal needs than the possession of a friend who meets every misfortune joyfully, so that, as the Apostle says, shoulder to shoulder, they bear one another's burdens. Even more—each one carries his own injuries even more lightly than that of his friend. Friendship, therefore, heightens the joys of prosperity and mitigates the sorrows of adversity by dividing and sharing them. Hence, the best medicine in life is a friend.

— ST. AELRED OF RIEVAULX (C. 1110 – 67)

To Blessed Diana d'Andalò

Beloved, since I cannot see you with my bodily eyes nor be consoled with your presence as often as you would wish and I would wish, it is at least some refreshment to me, some appeasement of my heart's longing, when I can visit you by means of my letters and tell you how things are with me, just as I long to know how things are with you, for your progress and your gaiety of heart are a sweet nourishment to my soul—though you for your part do not know to what ends of the earth I may be journeying and even if you knew you would not have messengers to hand by whom you could send something to me. Yet whatever we may write to each other matters little, beloved: within our hearts is the ardor of our love in the Lord whereby you speak to me and I to you continuously in those wordless outpourings of charity that no tongue can express nor letter contain.

O Diana, how unhappy this present condition of things that we must suffer: that we cannot love each other without pain and anxiety! You weep and are in bitter grief because it is not given you to see me continually; and I equally grieve that it is so rarely given me to be with you. . . .

These things we must bear with patience . . . , for with what measure our trials are meted to us, so shall be measured our joy, poured out on us by God's Son Jesus

Christ, to whom is honor and glory and strength and em-
pire forever and ever.

— BLESSED JORDAN OF SAXONY (C. 1190–1237)

To His Daughter

Mistrust him, Meg, will I not, though I feel me faint. Yea,
and though I should feel my fear even at point to over-
throw me too, yet shall I remember how St. Peter with a
blast of a wind began to sink for his faint faith, and shall do
as he did, call upon Christ and pray him to help. And then
I trust he shall set his holy hand unto me, and in the stormy
seas hold me up from drowning. Yea, and if he suffer me to
play St. Peter further, and to fall full to the ground, and
swear and forswear too (which our Lord for his tender passion keep me from, and let me lose if it so fall, and never
win thereby): yet after shall I trust that his goodness will
cast upon me his tender piteous eye, as he did upon St.
Peter, and make me stand up again, and confess the truth of
my conscience afresh, and abide the shame and the harm
here of mine own fault. And finally, Marget, this wot I very
well, that without my fault he will not let me be lost. . . .
And therefore, mine own good daughter, never trouble thy
mind, for anything that ever shall hap me in this world.
Nothing can come, but that that God will. . . . And if anything hap me that you would be loath, pray to God for me,
but trouble not yourself: as I shall full heartily pray for us
all, that we may meet together once in heaven, where we
shall make merry forever, and never have trouble after.

— ST. THOMAS MORE (1478–1535)

To St. Jane Frances de Chantal

In order to cut short all the rebuttals that may be taking shape in your mind, I must tell you that I have never understood that there was any bond between us carrying with it any obligation but that of charity and true Christian friendship, what St. Paul calls "the bond of perfection"; and truly, that is just what it is, for it is indissoluble and never weakens. All other bonds are temporal, even that of a vow of obedience, which can be broken through death or other circumstances; but the bond of love grows and gets ever stronger with time. It cannot be cut down by death, which, like a scythe, mows down everything but charity. "Love is strong as death and firm as hell," says Solomon. So there, dear sister (allow me to call you by this name, which is the one used by the apostles and the first Christians to express the intimate love they had for one another), this is our bond, these are our chains, which the more they are tightened and press against us, the more they bring us joy and freedom. Their strength is gentleness; their violence, mildness; nothing is more pliable than that; nothing, stronger. Think of me as very closely bound to you, and don't try to understand more about it than that this bond is not opposed to any other bond either of a vow or of marriage. Be totally at peace on that score. Obey your first director freely, and call on me in charity and sincerity.

— ST. FRANCIS DE SALES (1567–1622)

To Katharine Asquith

The Faith, the Catholic Church, is discovered, is recognized, triumphantly enters reality like a landfall at sea that at first was thought a cloud. The nearer it is seen, the more is it real, the less imaginary: the more direct and external its voice, the more indubitable its representative character, its "persona," its voice. The metaphor is not that men fall in love with it: the metaphor is that they discover home. "This was what I sought. This was my need." It is the very mold of the mind, the matrix to which corresponds in every outline the outcast and unprotected contour of the soul. It is Verlaine's "Oh! Rome—oh! Mère!" And that not only to those who had it in childhood and have returned, but much more—and what a proof!—to those who come upon it from over the hills of life and say to themselves "Here is the town."

— HILAIRE BELLOC (1870–1953)

To Maurice Bellière

I completely agree with you that "the heart of God is saddened more by the thousand little indelicacies of His friends than it is by the faults, even the grave ones, that people of the world commit." But my dear little brother, it seems to me that it is only when his friends, ignoring their continual indelicacies, make a habit out of them and don't ask forgiveness for them, that Jesus can utter those touching words that the Church puts on his lips in Holy Week: "These wounds you see in the palms of my hands are the ones I received in the house of those who loved me." For those who love Him, and after each fault come to ask pardon by throwing themselves into His arms, Jesus trembles with joy. He says to His angels what the father of the prodigal son said to his servants: "Put his best robe on him and put a ring on his finger, and let us rejoice." Ah! my brother, how the goodness of Jesus, His merciful love, are so little known! It is true that to enjoy these riches we must be humbled and recognize our nothingness, and that is what so many are not willing to do. But my little brother, that is not the way you behave, so the way of simple love and confidence is just made to order for you.

— ST. THÉRÈSE OF LISIEUX (1873 – 97)

Letter to Jesus

Dear Jesus,

I have been criticized. "He's a bishop, he's a cardinal," people have said, "he's been writing letters to all kinds of people: to Mark Twain, to Péguy, and heaven knows how many others. And not a line to Jesus Christ!"

Here is my letter. I write it trembling, feeling like a poor deaf mute trying to make himself understood. . . .

When you said: "Blessed are the poor, blessed are the persecuted," I wasn't with you. If I had been, I'd have whispered into your ear: "For heaven's sake, Lord, change the subject, if you want to keep any followers at all. Don't you know that everyone wants riches and comfort? Cato promised his soldiers the figs of Africa, Caesar promised his the riches of Gaul, and, for better or worse, the soldiers followed them. But you're promising poverty and persecution. Who do you think's going to follow you?" You went ahead unafraid, and I can hear you saying you were the grain of wheat that must die before it bears fruit; and that you must be raised upon a cross and from there draw the whole world up to you.

Today, this has happened: they raised you up on a cross. You took advantage of that to hold out your arms and draw people up to you. And countless people have come to the foot of the cross, to fling themselves into your arms.

— POPE JOHN PAUL I (1912 – 78)

Entering the Everlasting: Death into Life

Beyond death lies life with God. We cling to Jesus' promise to his disciples, "I am going to prepare a place for you" (Jn. 14:2). This is not simply unending existence but something much deeper, and more mysterious—a full participation in the life of God. This personal relationship with God has already begun in our earthly life of prayer, service, sacrament, and discipleship. After death, the relationship reaches its fullness. At its heart is divine love.

Suffering is unavoidable on the journey to the place that Jesus has prepared for us. Jesus accomplished our salvation through his suffering and death. In our journey with him through life we unite our own sufferings with his. "The mystery of Christ is the ultimate truth," said the monk Dom Bede Griffiths. "It is something that comes when we let go."

IN
WEAKNESS,
STRENGTH

After withdrawing about a stone's throw from them and kneeling, he prayed, saying, "Father, if you are willing, take this cup away from me; still, not my will but yours be done." [And to strengthen him an angel from heaven appeared to him. He was in such agony and he prayed so fervently that his sweat became like drops of blood falling on the ground.]

—LUKE 22:41–44

The Joyful Giver

It is not enough to help the poor. We must help them with generosity and without grumbling.

And it is not enough to help them without grumbling. We must help them gladly and happily.

When the poor are helped there ought to be these two conditions: generosity and joy.

Why do you complain of giving something to the poor? Why do you display bad temper in the practice of almsgiving? If they see you in that frame of mind, the poor would prefer to refuse your gift. If you give with a brusque demeanor, you are not being generous but lacking gentleness and courtesy. If your face reveals a feeling of hostility, you cannot bring comfort to your brother or sister who is living in the midst of hostility.

Afterward, you will be happy to see that they do not feel ashamed or humiliated just because you have helped them joyfully. Nothing actually causes shame so much as having to receive something from someone else.

By showing great joyfulness you will succeed in enabling your brother or sister to overcome their sensitivity. They will understand that in your opinion receiving is just as beautiful as giving.

By showing bad temper, on the other hand, far from cheering them up you will be depressing them even further.

If you give gladly, even if you give only a little, it is a big gift. If you give unwillingly, even if you give a big gift, you turn it into a small one.

— ST. JOHN CHRYSOSTOM (C. 349 – 407)

St. Frances of Rome

God tested the patience of Frances not only in the external events that happened to her, but it was also his will to try her in her body by many illnesses. It is a well-known fact that she was tried by long and serious illnesses. Yet she was never seen to show the slightest impatience, or the slightest dissatisfaction with any service done for her no matter how clumsily it was done.

Frances gave proof of her steadfastness when her sons, whom she dearly loved, died prematurely. She bowed to the will of God with serenity of spirit and gave him thanks for all that happened. That same steadfastness enabled her to endure the evil-tongued detractors who spoke ill of her way of life. Never did she show the slightest antipathy for those whom she knew spoke evil of her and of what she did. Instead, she repaid evil with good and prayed unceasingly to God for them.

God had chosen her for sanctity, not simply for her own sake, but so that she might direct his gifts to her toward the spiritual and bodily welfare of her neighbor. He gave her such an abundance of loving-kindness that anyone who had dealings with her immediately felt himself captivated by love and admiration for her and was ready to do whatever she wished.

(St. Frances of Rome: 1384–1440)

Learning from the Poor

There is a useful method for strengthening hearts that lack courage. This is to give them the privilege of seeing the poor, of being shown Our Lord Jesus Christ not only in holy pictures painted by great artists but of being shown Jesus Christ and his wounds in the person of the poor.

The sons of noblemen must learn what it means to be hungry and thirsty or to live in an attic without clothing or furniture. They must be able to see dire poverty in the guise of sick children, of children who are weeping. They must be able to see them and to love them.

— BLESSED ANTOINE FRÉDÉRIC OZANAM
(1813 – 53)

Serving by Suffering

In our eyes the poor man, whom we help, will never be the creature whom many consider useless. We believe that, by suffering, he is serving God and is therefore serving society just as much as someone who prays. In our eyes he is performing an act of reparation, a sacrifice that brings down graces on all of us. We have less confidence in the protection offered by a lightning conductor on the roof than in the prayer of the poor woman and her children who sleep on straw near the top of the building.

— BLESSED ANTOINE FRÉDÉRIC OZANAM
(1813 – 53)

Blessed Mary MacKillop

Mary was the eldest of eight children born to Scottish immigrants. Of her early years she writes: "My life as a child was one of sorrow, my home, when I had it, was a most unhappy one."

At sixteen Mary became the main provider and after some years started to teach in Penola in southeast Australia—a Church school where the education was free to all children. The success of the school was immediate. Mary was joined by other dedicated women and the Sisters of St. Joseph were formed—the first Order to be founded by an Australian.

However the more conservative Catholics were unsure of the vigorous new Order and some of the bishops found it impossible. The freshness of the vision and its practical interpretation were unsettling! The Bishop of

Adelaide declared Mary excommunicated and disbanded the Order. However the excommunication was ruled invalid and Mary's next step was to beg her passage to Rome where Pope Pius IX approved and blessed the Constitution of the Sisters.

On her return to Australia, shelters for the elderly and the homeless were opened. The schools spread through the bush and across to New Zealand. Mary died in Sydney and is known as the Australian People's Saint.

(Blessed Mary MacKillop: 1842–1909)

A Gold Chain

O Jesus, here I am before you. You are suffering and dying for me, old as I am now and drawing near the end of my service and my life. Hold me closely, and near to your heart, letting mine beat with yours. I love to feel myself bound forever to you with a gold chain, woven of lovely, delicate links.

The first link: the justice that obliges me to find my God wherever I turn.

The second link: the providence and goodness that will guide my feet.

The third link: love for my neighbor, unwearying and most patient.

The fourth link: the sacrifice that must always be my lot, and that I will and must welcome at all times.

The fifth link: the glory that Jesus promises me in this life and in eternity.

O crucified Jesus, "my love and my mercy now and forever." "Father, if thou art willing, remove this cup from me; nevertheless not my will, but thine be done" (Luke 22:42).

—POPE JOHN XXIII (1881–1963)

Seek What Unites

Love one another, my dear children.
Seek rather what unites,
Not what may separate you
    from one another.
As I take leave, or better still
As I say "till we meet again"
Let me remind you of the
    most important things in life.
Our blessed Savior Jesus; His good news;
His holy Church: truth and kindness. . . .
I shall remember you all
And pray for you.

—POPE JOHN XXIII (1881–1963)

Your Merciful Love

I often have the impression, and I hope I am not being presumptuous in thinking so, that Jesus keeps me as it were on a leash. There are times when I feel very strong and sure of myself, especially in public, and this is important in front of others. But there are other moments that those around me do not know of, when I am overwhelmed with a feeling of utter weakness and impotence. In these moments of

weakness when Jesus pulls upon the leash as it were, to remind me of my nothingness, I say to Him "Jesus, I abandon myself to Your Merciful Love" but I do not always say
it with complete and utter confidence. Pray then, my
beloved friend, that Jesus will give me the grace to believe,
that He will give me total faith, that He will never forsake
me. I am, as it were, like St. Peter trying to walk on the surface of the water. . . .

I can say only "May His Will be done." My tour of
duty as Governor-General [of Canada] is to be of five years'
duration. It will be for Jesus to decide how long I will be
able in weakness to serve Him and to serve my country.

— GEORGES P. VANIER (1888–1967)

Everyone Is Lovable

Love never gets out of date. Love, therefore, all things, and
all persons in God.

> So long as there are poor, I am poor;
> So long as there are prisons, I am a prisoner;
> So long as there are sick, I am weak;
> So long as there is ignorance, I must learn the truth;
> So long as there is hate, I must love;
> So long as there is hunger, I am famished.

Such is the identification Our Divine Lord would
have us make with all whom He made in love and for love.
Where we do not find love, we must put it. Then everyone
is lovable. There is nothing in all the world more calculated
to inspire love for others than this Vision of Christ in our
fellow man: "For I was hungry, and you gave me to eat;

I was thirsty, and you gave me to drink; I was a stranger, and you took me in; Naked, and you covered me; sick and you visited me; I was in prison, and you came to me."

— FULTON SHEEN (1895 – 1979)

The Hand of God

For me Jesus Christ is *everything*. . . . He was and he is my ideal from the moment of my entrance into the Society [of Jesus]. He was and he continues to be my way; he was and he still is my strength. I don't think it is necessary to explain very much what that means. Take Jesus Christ from my life and everything would collapse—like a human body from which someone removed the skeleton, heart, and head. . . .

In Lourdes, I acquired an awareness of the power of God as he intervenes in history.

In Marneffe, after our expulsion from Spain, I lived in a community of 350 persons who wondered each evening if they would have enough food for the following day. And each day, we had enough.

In the Yamaguchi prison, I was alone for thirty-five days, wondering why I was there, for how long, and if, in the end, I might be executed. When this "experience" was over, you could not help but believe in a special Providence.

And immediately after the explosion of the atomic bomb in Hiroshima—shouldn't I remember how we were able to feed and care for so many wounded?

When, in the following years, I traveled throughout the world seeking men and collecting funds for Japan, I was the witness to a rare generosity and to extraordinary sacrifices. One might give many reasons for this, but as for me, I saw in it the hand of God.

— PEDRO ARRUPE (1907–91)

Repentance

It seems a characteristic of one's later years that whilst the wrongs one has suffered fade in one's memory toward vanishing point, the wrongs one has inflicted on others stand out ever more distinctly. It is not that one is consumed with guilt over sins long since confessed but rather that the undoubted effects and the suspected effects of one's actions upon others really strike to the heart. But it is a joy-bringing revelation as well because it reveals how one's heart is longing as never before for repentance. Old age, therefore, as many cultures teach and as Christendom once knew, is the age of repentance. And in that joyful repentance there is also a deep poignancy because, inevitably, many of those one feels to have harmed, in one way or another, are dead. As a result direct reparation toward them is no longer possible. However the burning regret that one cannot now make reparation toward them only intensifies one's desire and determination to behave with all the more kindness and compassion toward anyone who comes across one's path during whatever time is left.

At the same time, if that desire and determination are not themselves to become a burdensome duty but a source of joy, then they have to be accompanied by a real hope that in some way our acts of kindness and compassion will, within the economy of salvation, touch those who have gone before us even though we ourselves can no longer touch them directly. That is a matter of hope—not of hopefulness.

— DONALD NICHOLL (1923 – 97)

To Love Deeply

Do not hesitate to love and to love deeply. You might be afraid of the pain that deep love can cause. When those you love deeply reject you, leave you, or die, your heart will be broken. But that should not hold you back from loving deeply. The pain that comes from deep love makes your love ever more fruitful. It is like a plow that breaks the ground to allow the seed to take root and grow into a strong plant. Every time you experience the pain of rejection, absence, or death, you are faced with a choice. You can become bitter and decide not to love again, or you can stand straight in your pain and let the soil on which you stand become richer and more able to give life to new seeds.

The more you have loved and have allowed yourself to suffer because of your love, the more you will be able to let your heart grow wider and deeper. When your love is truly giving and receiving, those whom you love will not leave your heart even when they depart from you. They will become part of your self and thus gradually build a community within you. . . . Yes, as you love deeply the ground of your heart will be broken more and more, but you will rejoice in the abundance of the fruit it will bear.

— HENRI J. M. NOUWEN (1932 – 96)

Love Me as You Are

I know your misery, the inner struggle of your heart. I also know the weaknesses of your heart. I am aware of your cowardice, your sins, and your falls. I still tell you "Love me as you are." If you wait to be an angel before you give me your love, you will never love me. Even if you often fall again into sins you are ashamed of, even if you are poor in the practice of virtue, I do not allow you not to love me. Love me as you are! Yes, give me your heart at all times and in whatever dispositions you may be, in fervor or in dryness, faithful or unfaithful, love me as you are. I want the love of your poor heart. If you want to be perfect before giving me your heart, you will never love me. What can prevent me from turning every grain of sand into a shining radiant archangel of great nobility? Don't you believe that I could bring into being thousands of saints, more perfect and loving than those I have created? Am I not the Almighty God? But if I choose to be loved, here and now, by your limited heart in preference to more perfect love . . . will you refuse . . . ? can you refuse . . . ?

MARTYRDOM

*L*et us beset the just one, because he is obnoxious
        to us;
    he sets himself against our doings,
Reproaches us for transgressions of the law
        and charges us with violations of our training.
He professes to have knowledge of God
        and styles himself a child of the LORD.
To us he is the censure of our thoughts;
        merely to see him is a hardship for us,
Because his life is not like other men's,
        and different are his ways.
He judges us debased;
        he holds aloof from our paths as from things
            impure.
He calls blest the destiny of the just
        and boasts that God is his Father.
Let us see whether his words be true;
        let us find out what will happen to him.
For if the just one be the son of God, he will defend
    him
        and deliver him from the hand of his foes.
With revilement and torture let us put him to the test
        that we may have proof of his gentleness
        and try his patience.

Let us condemn him to a shameful death;
  for according to his own words, God will take care
  of him."

—WISDOM 2:12–20

United in Death

The day of their victory dawned, and they made their way from the prison to the amphitheater, with cheerful faces and in dignified manner, as though they were on the way to heaven. If they were trembling at all, it was from joy, not fear.

Perpetua was first tossed by the cow and she fell on her back. Then she stood up, and when she saw that Felicity had been crushed to the ground, she went and gave her her hand to help her up; and so they stood, side by side. Now that the cruelty of the people was appeased, they were recalled to the Sanavivaria Gate. There Perpetua was supported by a certain Rusticus, a catechumen at that time, who was keeping close to her. She began to look around her, as though she had been roused from a sleep, so deeply had she been in spiritual ecstasy, and she said, to the astonishment of all, "When are we to be thrown to that cow or whatever it is?" And when she was told that this had already been done, she would not believe it until she noticed a number of marks of violence to her body and clothes. Then she summoned her brother and the catechumen, and spoke to them saying, "Stand firm in your faith, and love one another. Do not let your sufferings be a stumbling block to you."

Saturninus at another gate was also giving encouragement to Pudens, a soldier. "It has happened," he said, "exactly as I supposed and foretold. Up till now, I have not been touched by a beast. And now you can believe me with all your heart. I shall go forward there and with one bite of the leopard I shall be finished off."

—— • ——

And at once as the show was ending, Saturninus was thrown to the leopard, and with one bite was so drenched with blood that as he came back, the people called out in witness to his second baptism, "Well washed! well washed!" Indeed he was saved who had been washed in this fashion.

Then he said to Pudens, the soldier, "Farewell, and remember me and the faith. Do not let all this disturb you, but rather be strengthened by it." Then he asked for the ring from Pudens' finger. He dipped it in his wound, and gave it back to him for a legacy, as a pledge and memorial of his blood. Then he became unconscious, and was thrown with the others into the place where their throats were to be cut.

When the people demanded that they be brought into the open, to make themselves party to the murder by watching with their eyes the sword being plunged into the bodies, the Christians rose up of their own accord and crossed over to where the people wanted. Then they kissed each other, so that their martyrdom could be brought to fulfillment by the ritual kiss of peace. The rest of them received the sword without moving and in silence, especially Saturninus, who as the first to ascend, was the first to yield up his life. For he was waiting again for Perpetua. But Perpetua, that she might taste something of the pain, was struck on the bone, and she cried out. And she herself guided the fumbling hand of the novice gladiator into her throat. Perhaps such a woman could not be otherwise killed, a woman who was feared by an unclean spirit, unless she herself gave consent.

(St. Felicity and St. Perpetua: d. 203)

St. John Houghton and Companions

Early in the morning of May 4, 1535, a spectacle was witnessed inside the gates of the Tower of London, never before seen in the history of England, or of any Christian country in Europe. Three monks in their white habits were being led out from their prisons, to be dragged on hurdles to the place of execution at Tyburn. They were very cheerful. Thomas More, looking out from the window of his cell, turned to his daughter, Margaret, who was visiting him at the time, and said: "Lo, dost thou not see, Meg, that these blessed Fathers be now as cheerfully going to their deaths as bridegrooms to their marriage?"

Campion's Brag

Touching our Society, be it known to you that we have made a league—all the Jesuits in the world, whose succession and multitude must overreach all the practices of England—cheerfully to carry the cross you shall lay upon us, and never to despair your recovery, while we have a man left to enjoy your Tyburn, or to be racked with your torments, or consumed with your prisons. The expense is reckoned, the enterprise is begun; it is of God, it cannot be withstood. So the faith was planted: so it must be restored.

— ST. EDMUND CAMPION (1540 – 81)

St. Paul Miki and Companions

When the crosses had been erected, it was wonderful to see how steadfast all were in response to the encouragement given by Father Pasius and Father Rodríguez. Father Commissarius remained almost immobile, his eyes fixed on heaven. Brother Martin continually gave thanks to God, singing psalms with the versicle, "Into your hands, O Lord." Brother Francis Blanco also gave thanks to God in a loud voice, while Father Gonsalvez, raising his voice a little, recited the Lord's Prayer and the Hail Mary.

Our brother, Paul Miki, seeing that he was standing in the most honored pulpit of any he had ever been in, first of all declared to the onlookers that he was both a Japanese and a Jesuit. He told them that he was dying because he had preached the gospel, and that he gave thanks to God for such a singular privilege. Then he added the following words, "Since I have now come to this moment, I do not think there is anyone among you who would believe that I would willingly tell a lie. I tell you openly, then, that there is no other way of salvation than that of the Christians. Since that way teaches me to forgive my enemies and all who have done me violence, I willingly forgive the king and those who have a hand in my death, and I entreat them to seek the initiation of Christian baptism."

Then, looking to his companions, he began to encourage them in this last agony. On the face of each of them there appeared a great joy, and this was especially true of Louis. When one of the other Christians cried out that soon he would be in Paradise, he responded with such a joyful movement of his hands and his whole body that he attracted the attention of all the onlookers.

Anthony, who was beside Louis, with his eyes fixed on heaven, called on the most holy names of Jesus and Mary, and then sang the psalm, *Laudate, pueri, Dominum.* He had learned this at the catechetical school in Nagasaki, for among the tasks given to the children there had been included the learning of some psalms such as these.

The others kept repeating, "Jesus, Mary," and their faces showed no sign of distress. Some of them, indeed, were encouraging the bystanders to lead good Christian lives. By these actions and by others like them, they gave ample proof of their willingness to die.

Then the four executioners began to take their spears out of the sheaths that the Japanese use. When they saw those terrible spears, all the faithful cried out, "Jesus, Mary." What is more, a sad lamentation assailed heaven itself. The executioners dispatched each of them in a very short time with one or two thrusts.

(St. Paul Miki: d. 1597)

Martyrdom of Love

One day St. Jane said this: "My dear daughters, most of our holy Fathers, the pillars of the Church, were not martyrs. Why was this, do you think?"

After each one of us had had her say, she went on: "I think it is because there is such a thing as a martyrdom of love: God keeps his servants alive to work for his glory, and this makes them martyrs and confessors at the same time. I know this is the sort of martyrdom the daughters of the Visitation will suffer, that is, those of them who are fortunate enough to set their hearts on it."

A sister wanted to know just how this martyrdom worked out in practice.

"Give God your unconditional consent," she said, "and then you will find out. What happens is that love seeks out the most intimate and secret place of your soul, as with a sharp sword, and cuts you off even from your own self. I know of a soul cut off in this way so that she felt it more keenly than if a tyrant had cleaved her body from her soul."

We knew, of course, that she was speaking about herself.

———•———

A sister wanted to know how long this martyrdom was likely to last.

"From the moment we give ourselves up wholeheartedly to God until the moment we die," she answered. "But this goes for generous hearts and people who keep faith with love and don't take back their offering; our Lord doesn't take the trouble to make martyrs of feeble hearts and people who have little love and not much constancy; he just lets them jog along in their own little way in case they give up and slip from his hands altogether; he never forces our free will."

She was asked whether this martyrdom of love could ever be as bad as the physical kind.

"We won't try to compare the two and look for equality; but I do not think the martyrdom of love is less painful than the other, because 'love is strong as death,' and martyrs of love suffer infinitely more by staying alive to do God's will than if they had to give up a thousand lives for their faith and love and loyalty."

— FROM THE MEMOIR OF A SECRETARY FOR ST. JANE FRANCES DE CHANTAL (1572–1641)

The Korean Martyrs, 1784–1839

The Christian community in Korea is unique in the history of the Church by reason of the fact that it was founded entirely by laypeople. In less than a century [from 1784] it could already boast some ten thousand martyrs from the thirteen-year-old Peter Yu to the seventy-two-year-old Mark Chong. Men and women, clergy and laity, rich and poor, ordinary people and nobles, many of them descendants of earlier unsung martyrs—they all gladly died for the sake of Christ.

Listen to the last words of Teresa Kwon, one of the early martyrs: "Since the Lord of heaven is the Father of all mankind and the Lord of all creation, how can you ask me to betray him? Even in this world anyone who betrays his own father or mother will not be forgiven. All the more may I never betray him who is the Father of us all."

And what did the seventeen-year-old Agnes Yi say when she and her younger brother were falsely told that their parents had betrayed the faith? "Whether my parents betrayed or not is their affair. As for us, we cannot betray the Lord of heaven whom we have always served." Hearing this, six other adult Christians freely delivered themselves to the magistrate to be martyred. Agnes, her parents, and those other six are all being canonized today. In addition, there are countless other unknown humble martyrs who no less faithfully and bravely served the Lord.

— POPE JOHN PAUL II (B. 1920)

The Uganda Martyrs, 1885–87

"Who are these clothed in white robes, and whence have they come?" (Revelation 7:13). This verse of scripture comes to mind as we add to the glorious list of saints triumphant in heaven these twenty-two sons of Africa. Who are they? They are Africans, first of all. By their color, race, and culture they are true Africans, descended from the Bantu race and the peoples of the Upper Nile.

Yes, they are Africans and they are martyrs. "These are they who have come out of the great tribulation." Twenty-two martyrs were recognized but there were many more and not only Catholics. There were also Anglicans and some Muslims.

— POPE PAUL VI (1897–1978)

The Seed of Liberty

I have often been threatened with death. I have to say, as a Christian, that I don't believe in death without resurrection: if they kill me, I will rise again in the Salvadorean people. I tell you this without any boasting, with the greatest humility. As pastor, I am obliged, by divine command, to give my life for those I love, who are all Salvadoreans, even for those who are going to assassinate me. If the threats are carried out, even now I offer my blood to God for the redemption and resurrection of El Salvador. Martyrdom is a grace of God I don't think I deserve. But if God accepts the sacrifice of my life, may my blood be the seed of liberty and the sign that hope will soon become reality. May my death, if accepted by God, be for the freedom of my people and as a witness to hope in the future. You can say, if they come to kill me, that I forgive and bless those who do it. Hopefully they may realize that they will be wasting their time. A bishop will die, but the Church of God, which is the people, will never perish.

— OSCAR ROMERO (1917– 80)

"A-Dieu"

When an *"A-Dieu"* takes on a face.
If it should happen one day—and it could be today—
that I become a victim of the terrorism which now
    seems ready to engulf
all the foreigners living in Algeria,

I would like my community, my Church, my family,
to remember that my life was *given* to God and to this
  country.
I ask them to accept that the Sole Master of all life
was not a stranger to this brutal departure.
I ask them to pray for me—
for how could I be found worthy of such an offering?
I ask them to be able to link this death with the many
  other deaths
which were just as violent, but forgotten through
  indifference and anonymity.
My life has no more value than any other.
Nor any less value.
In any case it has not the innocence of childhood.
I have lived long enough to know that I am an
  accomplice in the evil
which seems, alas, to prevail in the world,
even in that which would strike me blindly.
I should like, when the time comes, to have the
  moment of lucidity
which would allow me to beg forgiveness of God
and of my fellow human beings,
and at the same time to forgive with all my heart the
  one who would strike
me down.

           — CHRISTIAN DE CHERGÉ (1937–96)

DEATH AND ETERNITY

*D*o not let your hearts be troubled. You have faith
in God; have faith also in me. In my Father's
house there are many dwelling places. If there were not,
would I have told you that I am going to prepare a
place for you? And if I go and prepare a place for you,
I will come back again and take you to myself, so that
where I am you also may be.

—JOHN 14:1–3

Ground by Lions' Teeth

For my part, I am writing to all the churches and assuring
them that I am truly in earnest about dying for God—if
only you yourselves put no obstacles in the way. I must implore you to do me no such untimely kindness; pray leave
me to be a meal for the beasts, for it is they who can provide my way to God. I am his wheat, ground fine by the
lions' teeth to be made purest bread for Christ. So intercede with him for me, that by their instrumentality I may
be made a sacrifice to God.

All the ends of the earth, all the kingdoms of the world
would be of no profit to me; so far as I am concerned, to

die in Jesus Christ is better than to be monarch of earth's widest bounds. He who died for us is all that I seek; he who rose again for us is my whole desire. The pangs of birth are upon me; have patience with me, my brothers, and do not shut me out from life, do not wish me to be stillborn. Here is one who only longs to be God's; do not make a present of him to the world again, or delude him with the things of earth. Suffer me to attain to light, light pure and undefiled; for only when I am come thither shall I be truly a man. Leave me to imitate the passion of my God. If any of you has God within himself, let that man understand my longings, and feel for me, because he will know the forces by which I am constrained.

———•———

It is the hope of this world's prince to get hold of me and undermine my resolve, set as it is upon God. Pray let none of you lend him any assistance, but take my part instead, for it is the part of God. Do not have Jesus Christ on your lips, and the world in your heart; do not cherish thoughts of grudging me my fate. Even if I were to come and implore you in person, do not yield to my pleading; keep your compliance for this written entreaty instead. Here and now, as I write in the fullness of life, I am yearning for death with all the passion of a lover. Earthly longings have been crucified; in me there is left no spark of desire for mundane things, but only a murmur of living water that whispers within me, "Come to the Father." There is no pleasure for me in any meats that perish, or in the delights of this life; I am fain for the bread of God, even the flesh of Jesus Christ, who is the seed of David; and for my drink I crave that blood of his that is love imperishable.

I want no more of what men call life. And my want can come true, if it is your desire. Pray, then, let it be your desire; so that in your turn you also may be desired. Not to write at more length, I appeal to you to believe me. Jesus Christ will make it clear to you that I am speaking the truth; he is a faithful mouthpiece, by which the Father's words of truth find utterance. Intercede for me, then, that I may have my wish; for I am not writing now as a mere man, but I am voicing the mind of God. My suffering will be a proof of your goodwill; my rejection, a proof of your disfavor.

— ST. IGNATIUS OF ANTIOCH (C. 35 – C. 107)

Farewell

But because the day when my mother was to quit this life was drawing near—a day known to you, though we were ignorant of it—she and I happened to be alone, through the mysterious workings of your will, as I believe. We stood leaning against a window that looked out on a garden within the house where we were staying at Ostia on the Tiber, for there, far from the crowds, we were recruiting our strength after the long journey, in preparation for our voyage overseas. We were alone, conferring very intimately. Forgetting what lay in the past, and stretching out to what was ahead, we inquired between ourselves in the light of the present truth, the Truth that is yourself, what the eternal life of the saints would be like. Eye has not seen nor ear heard nor human heart conceived it, yet with the mouth of our hearts wide open we panted thirstily for the celestial streams of your fountain, the fount of life that is with you, that bedewed from it according to our present capacity we might in our little measure think upon a thing so great.

— ST. AUGUSTINE OF HIPPO (354 – 430)

The Seventh Day

After this age God shall rest as on the seventh day, when God shall make that same seventh day that we shall be, to rest in Himself. Furthermore it would take up a long time to discourse now exactly of every one of those several ages. But this seventh shall be our sabbath, whose end shall not be the evening, but the Lord's day, as the eighth eternal day, which is sanctified and made holy by the resurrection of Christ, prefiguring not only the eternal rest of the spirit, but also of the body. There we shall rest and see, we shall see and love, we shall love, and we shall praise. Behold what shall be in the end without end! For what other thing is our end, but to come to that kingdom of which there is no end?

— ST. AUGUSTINE OF HIPPO (354 – 430)

Hope of the World

O God that art the only hope of the world,
The only refuge for unhappy men,
Abiding in the faithfulness of heaven,
Give me strong succor in this testing place.
O King, protect Thy man from utter ruin
Lest the weak faith surrender to the tyrant,

Facing innumerable blows alone.
Remember I am dust, and wind, and shadow,
And life as fleeting as the flower of grass.
But may the eternal mercy which hath shone
From time of old
Rescue Thy servant from the jaws of the lion.
Thou who didst come from on high in the cloak of flesh,
Strike down the dragon with that two-edged sword,
Whereby our mortal flesh can war with the winds
And beat down strongholds, with our Captain God.

— ATTRIBUTED TO ST. BEDE THE VENERABLE
(C. 673–735)

Before Thy Face Forever

I pray Thee, merciful Jesus, that as Thou hast graciously granted me sweet draughts from the Word, which tells of Thee, so wilt Thou, of Thy goodness, grant that I may come at length to Thee, the fount of all wisdom, and stand before Thy face forever.

— ST. BEDE THE VENERABLE (C. 673–735)

To His Mother

Not long will last that separation: there we shall see one another again and be happy without ever growing tired, united together with our Redeemer, praising Him with all our strength, and singing forever His mercies. I do not at all doubt that, leaving aside all that the reasoning of human nature says, we shall easily open the door to faith and to that simple and pure obedience to which we are held by God, offering Him freely and promptly that which is His, and all the more willingly the dearer to you is the thing that He takes from you, believing firmly that what God does is all of it well done, taking away what He first had given us, and for no other reason than to put it in a safe and sure place, and to give to it what we all desire for ourselves. I have said all this for no other reason than to satisfy the desire I have that Your Most Illustrious Ladyship and all my family may receive this my departure as a dear gift, and that you may accompany me and help me with your Mother's blessing to pass this gulf and reach the shore of all my hopes. I have done it with all the better will because I have nothing else left with which to give you some little proof of the love and filial reverence that I owe you. I end by asking once more very humbly for your blessing.

— ST. ALOYSIUS GONZAGA (1568 – 91)

The Fullness of Love

The mystery of Christ is the ultimate truth, the reality toward which all human life aspires. And this mystery is known by love. Love is going out of oneself, surrendering the self, letting the reality, the truth, take over. . . . It is not something we achieve for ourselves. It is something that comes when we let go. We have to abandon everything— all words, thoughts, hopes, fears, all attachment to ourselves or to any earthly things, and let the divine mystery take possession of our lives. It feels like death, and it is, in fact, a sort of dying. It is encountering the darkness, the abyss, the void. It is facing absolute nothingness—or as Augustine Baker, the English Benedictine, said, it is "the union of the nothing with the Nothing." This is the negative aspect of contemplation. The positive aspect is, of course, the opposite. It is total fulfillment, total wisdom, total bliss, the answer to all problems, the peace that passes understanding, the joy that is the fullness of love.

— BEDE GRIFFITHS (1906 – 93)

Mystery

The meaning of things, and their purpose
is in part now hidden
but shall in the end become clear.
The choice is between
the Mystery and the absurd.
To embrace the Mystery
is to discover the real.
It is to walk toward the light,
to glimpse the morning star, to catch sight
from time to time
of what is truly real
it is no more than a flicker of light
through the cloud of unknowing,
a fitful ray of light
that is a messenger from the sun
which is hidden from the gaze.
You see the light but not the sun.
When you set yourself to look more closely,
you will begin to see more sense
in the darkness that surrounds you.

Your eyes will begin to pick out
the shape of things and persons around you.
You will begin to see in them
the presence of the One
who gives them meaning and purpose,
and that it is He
who is the explanation of them all.

— BASIL HUME (1923 – 99)

Shouting Hallelujah

Ruby Turpin lifted her head. There was only a purple streak in the sky, cutting through a field of crimson and leading, like an extension of the highway, into the descending dusk. She raised her hands from the side of the pen in a gesture hieratic and profound. A visionary light settled in her eyes. She saw the streak as a vast swinging bridge extending upward from the earth through a field of living fire. Upon it a vast horde of souls were rumbling toward heaven. There were whole companies of white-trash, clean for the first time in their lives, and bands of black niggers in white robes, and battalions of freaks and lunatics shouting and clapping and leaping like frogs. And bringing up the end of the procession was a tribe of people whom she recognized at once as those who, like herself and Claud, had always had a little of everything and the God-given wit to use it right. She leaned forward to observe them closer. They were marching behind the others with great dignity, accountable as they had always been for good order and common sense and respectable behavior. They alone were on key. Yet she could see by their shocked and altered faces that even their virtues were being burned away. She lowered her hands and gripped the rail of the hog pen, her eyes small but fixed unblinkingly on what lay ahead. In a moment the vision faded but she remained where she was, immobile.

At length she got down and turned off the faucet and made her slow way on the darkening path to the house. In the woods around her the invisible cricket choruses had struck up, but what she heard were the voices of the souls climbing upward into the starry field and shouting hallelujah.

— FLANNERY O'CONNOR (1925 – 64)

A New Heaven and a New Earth

Then I saw a new heaven and a new earth. The former heaven and the former earth had passed away, and the sea was no more. I also saw the holy city, a new Jerusalem, coming down out of heaven from God, prepared as a bride adorned for her husband. I heard a loud voice from the throne saying, "Behold, God's dwelling is with the human race. He will dwell with them and they will be his people and God himself will always be with them [as their God]. He will wipe every tear from their eyes, and there shall be no more death or mourning, wailing or pain, [for] the old order has passed away."

— REVELATION 21:1– 4

SOURCES

Preface

p. xii *Best of Both Worlds,* by Bernard Basset (Burns and Oates, 1963); *God of Surprises,* by Gerard W. Hughes (Darton, Longman and Todd, 1985 and 1996).

Father, Son, and Holy Spirit

p. 4 St. Basil the Great. From the treatise "On the Holy Spirit," chap. 9.

p. 5 St. Columbanus. From Instruction 1 on Faith, "Sancti Columbani Opera."

p. 5 St. Hildegard of Bingen. "To the Trinity be praise!" is from *Symphonia: A Critical Edition of the Symphonia Armonie Celestium Revelationum,* trans. Barbara Newman (Ithaca, N.Y.: Cornell University Press, 1988).

p. 6 St. Hildegard of Bingen. "The Holy Spirit is life that gives life" is from *Hildegard of Bingen: An Anthology,* trans. Robert Carver, ed. Fiona Bowie and Oliver Davies (London: Society for Promoting Christian Knowledge, 1990).

p. 7 Richard of St. Victor. From book 3 of *The Trinity* (New York: Paulist Press, 1979), taken from *The Twelve Patriarchs, The Mystical Ark, Book Three of the Trinity,* trans. Grover A. Zinn, Classics of Western Spirituality (New York: Paulist Press, 1979).

p. 8 Dante Alighieri. From canto 33 of *Paradiso,* in *Dante's Paradise,* trans. Mark Musa (Bloomington: Indiana University Press, 1984).

p. 9 Julian of Norwich. From *Revelations of Divine Love,* chap. 59, taken from *All Shall Be Well,* by Sheila Upjohn (Darton, Longman and Todd, 1992).

p. 10 St. Catherine of Siena. From *The Dialogues of Catherine of Siena on Divine Revelation,* chap. 167.

p. 11 Blessed Elizabeth of the Trinity. From *Your Presence Is My Joy,* trans. the Darlington Carmel (Carmelite Convent, Nunnery Lane, Darlington, DL3 7PN, England).

God's Love for Us

p. 13 St. Gregory of Nyssa. From *On the Song of Songs,* chap. 2.

p. 14 St. Gertrude the Great. From *The Herald of Divine Love: Gertrude of Helfta,* trans. Margaret Winkworth, Classics of Western Spirituality (New York: Paulist Press, 1993).

p. 15 Julian of Norwich. From *Revelations of Divine Love,* chaps. 5, 86, taken from *All Shall Be Well,* by Sheila Upjohn (Darton, Longman and Todd, 1992).

p. 16 St. Catherine of Siena. From *The Dialogue,* trans. Suzanne Noffke, Classics of Western Spirituality (New York: Paulist Press, 1980).

p. 17 St. John of the Cross. From *Centred on Love: The Poems of St. John of the Cross,* trans. Marjorie Flower, O.C.D. (© 1983 The Carmelite Community, St. Andrew's Road, Varroville, NSW 2565, Australia), reproduced in *The Impact of God,* by Iain Matthew, O.C.D. (Hodder, 1995).

p. 18 Fulton Sheen. From *Lift Up Your Heart,* by Fulton Sheen (Burns and Oates, 1950).

Our Love for God

p. 20 St. Basil the Great. From *The Longer Rules of St. Basil the Great,* taken from *The Ascetic Works of St. Basil,* trans. Lowther Clarke (SPCK, 1925).

p. 21 St. Augustine of Hippo. From *The Confessions of St. Augustine,* chap. X: 27:38, trans. Maria Boulding (Hodder, 1997).

p. 21 Baldwin of Canterbury. From the treatises of Baldwin of Canterbury, treatise 10.

p. 22 St. Bonaventure. From the works of St. Bonaventure, opusc. 3, 29–30, 47.

p. 23 Attributed to St. Ignatius of Loyola. "Teach us, good Lord, to serve Thee" is commonly attributed to St. Ignatius.

p. 23 St. Ignatius of Loyola. "Take, Lord, and receive all my liberty" is from *The Spiritual Exercises of St. Ignatius,* trans. Louis J. Puhl (Chicago: Loyola University Press, 1951).

p. 24 St. John of the Cross. From a letter to Madre Leonor de San Gabriel, 8 July 1589, taken from *Lamps of Fire: Daily Readings with St. John of the Cross,* ed. Elizabeth Ruth Obbard, O.C.D. (Darton, Longman and Todd, 1985).

p. 25 Charles de Foucauld.

p. 25 Fulton Sheen. From *Go to Heaven* (Catholic Book Club).

p. 26 Bernard Lonergan. From *Method in Theology* (Darton, Longman and Todd, 1972).

p. 27 A Carthusian. From *The Wound of Love* (Darton, Longman and Todd, 1994).

Love of Neighbor

p. 30 St. John Chrysostom. From the homilies of St. John Chrysostom, homily 50.3.4.

p. 31 St. Augustine of Hippo. From St. Augustine's treatises on St. John, treatise 17:7–9.

p. 32 St. Caesarius of Arles. From the sermons of St. Caesarius of Arles, sermon 25.1.

p. 33 St. Bonaventure. From *The Life of St. Francis,* by St. Bonaventure, this translation taken from *Bonaventure,* trans. Ewert Cousins, Classics of Western Spirituality (New York: Paulist Press, 1978).

p. 34 St. Catherine of Siena. From a letter to Bartolomeo Dominici, in *The Letters of Catherine of Siena,* vol. I, trans. Suzanne Noffke (New York: Paulist Press, 1988).

p. 35 St. Teresa of Ávila. From *The Way of Perfection,* by Teresa of Jesus, chap. 41, par. 7–8, taken from *Living Water: Daily Readings with*

St. Teresa of Ávila, ed. Sister Mary, O.D.C. (Darton, Longman and Todd, 1986).

p. 36 St.Vincent de Paul. From the writings of St.Vincent de Paul, ep. 2546.

p. 37 Jean-Pierre de Caussade. From *The Flame of Divine Love: Daily Readings with Jean-Pierre de Caussade,* ed. Robert Llewelyn (1984).

p. 37 Blessed Joseph de Veuster. From a letter to his brother Father Pamphile, November 1873, reproduced in *The Heart of Father Damien, 1840–1889,* by Vital Jourdan, S.S.C.C., trans. Francis Larkin and Charles Davenport (Milwaukee: Bruce Publishing Company, 1955).

p. 38 St. Thérèse of Lisieux. Original source *Autobiography of St. Thérèse of Lisieux,* Ms C 15v, taken from *By Love Alone: Daily Readings with St. Thérèse of Lisieux,* ed. Michael Hollings (Darton, Longman and Todd, 1986).

p. 39 Dorothy Day. From *Dorothy Day, Selected Writings: By Little and by Little,* ed. Robert Ellsberg (Maryknoll, N.Y.: Orbis Books, 1992).

p. 39 Dorothy Day. From *The Long Loneliness: The Autobiography of Dorothy Day* (San Francisco: Harper and Row, 1952).

p. 40 Father David Gibbs. From a letter of Father David Gibbs, quoted in *Strange Vagabond of God: The Story of John Bradburne,* by John Dove, S.J. (Gracewing, 1997).

God the Creator

p. 44 St. Basil the Great. From *St. Basil on Prayer* II.5, reproduced in *The Sunday Sermons of the Great Fathers,* vol. 2 (London and New York: Longmans Green, 1958). © M. F. Toal, Esq.

p. 45 Traditional Celtic blessing. From *Celtic Spirituality and Nature,* by Dr. Mary Low (Edinburgh and Belfast: Blackstaff Press), taken from *Carmina Gadelica,* vol. I, by Alexander Carmichael (Scottish Academic Press, 22 Montgomery St., Edinburgh), p. 231. Copyright is vested in Trustees of Professor J. C. Watson, 1972.

p. 45 St. Hildegard of Bingen. "You, all-accomplishing" is from *Symphonia: A Critical Edition of the Symphonia Armonie Celestium Revelationum,* trans. Barbara Newman (Ithaca, N.Y.: Cornell University Press, 1988).

p. 46 St. Hildegard of Bingen. "Love" is from *Hildegard of Bingen: An Anthology,* trans. Robert Carver, ed. Fiona Bowie and Oliver Davies (SPCK, 1990).

p. 47 St. Francis of Assisi. From *Francis and Clare: The Complete Works,* trans. Regis J. Armstrong and Ignatius C. Brady, Classics of Western Spirituality (New York: Paulist Press, 1982).

p. 48 St. Thomas Aquinas. From Sermon on the Apostles Creed 13–14. English translation in *The Three Greatest Prayers* (Westminster, Md.: Newman Press, 1956).

p. 48 St. Thomas Aqunias. From *Summa Theologica,* pt. I.q.47.

p. 49 The Huron. From a letter written to Pope Pius XI in 1872, reproduced in *A Procession of Saints,* by James Brodrick, S.J. (Catholic Book Club, 1947).

p. 49 Gerard Manley Hopkins.

p. 50 Friedrich von Hügel. From *Essays and Addresses on the Philosophy of Religion,* vol. I (1921), reproduced in *Spiritual Counsels and Letters of Baron Friedrich von Hügel,* ed. Douglas V. Steere (Darton, Longman and Todd, 1964).

p. 51 Francis Thompson.

p. 52 Charles Péguy. From *Le Porche de la deuxieme vertu: Le mystere des Saints Innocents.* Translation © Dame Teresa Rodrigues, O.S.B., Stanbrook Abbey.

p. 52 Pierre Teilhard de Chardin. From *Hymn of the Universe,* by Pierre Teilhard de Chardin, English translation (New York: Harper and Row, 1965). © Georges Borchardt, Inc.

p. 53 Tony Walsh. From "A Statement," in *Alone for Others: The Life of Tony Walsh,* by Lucien Miller (Community Concerns Associates, 1987).

Jesus Born

p. 55 St. Ephraem the Syrian. From *Ephrem the Syrian: Hymns,* trans. Kathleen E. McVey, Classics of Western Spirituality (New York: Paulist Press, 1989). This section from Hymns on the Nativity 3.

p. 56 St. Augustine of Hippo. From an unidentified Australian translation of sermon 191.

p. 58 St. Leo the Great. From the letters of Pope St. Leo the Great, ep. 31, 2–3.

p. 58 St. Anselm of Canterbury. Prayer to St. Paul from *The Prayers and Meditations of St. Anselm,* trans. Sister Benedicta Ward, S.L.G. (Penguin, 1973).

p. 59 St. Robert Southwell.

p. 60 Pierre Teilhard de Chardin. From *Hymn of the Universe,* by Pierre Teilhard de Chardin, English translation (New York: Harper and Row, 1965). © Georges Borchardt, Inc.

p. 61 St. Edith Stein. From *The Writings of Edith Stein,* trans. Hilda Graef (New York: Paulist Press).

p. 62 Caryll Houselander.

p. 63 Raymond E. Brown. From *An Adult Christ at Christmas: Essays on the Three Biblical Christmas Stories,* by Raymond E. Brown (Collegeville, Minn.: Liturgical Press, 1977).

Jesus Crucified and Risen

p. 67 From "An Ancient Homily for Holy Saturday."

p. 68 St. Melito of Sardis. From a reading from the homily of Melito of Sardis on the Pasch, nn. 65–71, © The Editor, *The Way,* for Edward Maltesta (trans.) "Homily of Melito of Sardis on the Pasch," nn. 65–71: from *The Way,* vol. 2, no. 2, April 1962.

p. 69 St. Ephraem the Syrian. From Sermon on Our Lord 3:4–9.

p. 71 Paschal proclamation. From the liturgy on Holy Saturday night. © Rite of *Holy Week* © 1972 International Committee on English in the Liturgy, Inc.

p. 73 St. Andrew of Crete. From Homily Or. 10.

p. 74 "The Dream of the Rood." Authorship of "The Dream of the Rood" has been unknown for more than one thousand years. This version was taken by Stanbrook from J. A. W. Bennett's *Poetry of the Passion 1982.*

p. 76 St. Catherine of Siena. From *The Prayers of Catherine of Siena,* ed. Suzanne Noffke (New York: Paulist Press, 1983).

p. 77 Charles Péguy. From *Le Porche de la deuxieme vertu: Le mystere des Saints Innocents.* Translation © Dame Teresa Rodrigues, O.S.B., Stanbrook Abbey.

p. 79 Karl Rahner. From *The Eternal Year* (London: Burns and Oates, 1964).

The Coming of the Spirit

p. 84 Third Eucharistic Prayer. From the New English translation of the *Order of Mass and Eucharistic Prayers.* © 1969 International Committee on English in the Liturgy, Inc.

p. 85 Diadochus of Photice. From *Spiritual Works,* 23 (SC 5b), taken from *A Patristic Breviary,* by Thomas Spidlik, trans. Paul Drake (London: New City Press, 1992).

p. 86 Isaac of Nineveh. From *Isaac of Syria,* trans. Sebastian Brock, ed. A. M. Allchin (Darton, Longman and Todd, 1989).

p. 87 Bianco da Siena. Trans. R. F. Littledale, 1833–90.

p. 88 St. Mary Magdalen Dei Pazzi. From her writings *On Revelation* and *On Temptation.*

p. 88 Gerard Manley Hopkins.

p. 90 Paul Claudel. From the preface to *The Satin Slipper,* by Paul Claudel, trans. John O'Connor (London: Sheed and Ward, 1931). The preface was written by Paul Claudel in French and in English.

Our Lady

p. 93 St. Cyril of Alexandria. From the letters of St. Cyril of Alexandria, ep. 1.

p. 94 Cynewulf.

p. 95 St. Hildegard of Bingen.

p. 96 St. Aelred of Rievaulx. From Sermon 20.

p. 98 Dante Alighieri. Trans. Ronald Knox.

p. 98 Blessed John Duns Scotus. Cited by Berand de S. Maurice in *Duns Scotus.*

p. 99 Blessed John Duns Scotus. From Opus Oxoniensus III, 20.10, by permission of the Abbot of Nunraw.

p. 100 Julian of Norwich. From *Revelations of Divine Love,* chap. 60, taken from *All Shall Be Well,* by Sheila Upjohn (Darton, Longman and Todd, 1992).

p. 100 St. Louis Grignion de Montfort. From "God Alone" in *The Collected Writings of St. Louis Marie de Montfort* (Bay Shore, N.Y.: Montfort Publications, 1987).

p. 102 St. Bernadette of Lourdes. From a letter of St. Bernadette of Lourdes.

p. 103 Henri J. M. Nouwen. From "Mary, Mother of Priests" from an address delivered in Toronto.

Saints and Angels

p. 105 "St. Martin of Tours Shares His Cloak." From *A Select Library of the Nicene and Post-Nicene Fathers of the Christian Church,* vol. XI (Grand Rapids, Mich.: William B. Eerdmans, reprinted January 1973).

p. 106 St. Gregory of Nazianzus. From *Oration* 28, trans. L. Wickham and F. Williams.

p. 108 St. Patrick. From *The Confession of St. Patrick,* taken from Confession 34, 36, 37, 38, 39.

p. 109 Pseudo-Dionysius the Areopagite. From *The Celestial Hierarchy* (New York: Paulist Press, 1987).

p. 110 St. Adamnan of Iona. From *Life of Columba,* by Adamnan, pref. II and bk. III.

p. 111 St. Gregory the Great. From the homilies of Pope St. Gregory the Great on the Gospels, homily 34.8–9.

p. 112 Baldwin of Canterbury. From tractate 15 in *Spiritual Tractates: Baldwin of Ford,* trans. D. N. Bell (Kalamazoo, Mich.: Cistercian Publications, 1986).

p. 114 "St. Dominic, Herald of the Gospel." From selected sources of the history of the Order of Preachers.

p. 115 St. Francis de Sales. From *Daily Readings with St. Francis de Sales* (CTS, 1911).

p. 115 Pope John XXIII. From the homily of Pope John XXIII for the canonization of St. Martin de Porres, 6 May 1962.

p. 116 Diana Dewar. From *Saint of Auschwitz,* by Diana Dewar (Darton, Longman and Todd, 1982), slightly edited.

Church and Sacraments

p. 121 "Instructions to the Newly Baptized at Jerusalem."

p. 123 Letter to Diognetus. From the Letter to Diognetus, N 5–6.

p. 124 St. Boniface. From the letters of St. Boniface, letter 78.

p. 125 St. Thomas Aquinas. From the works of St. Thomas Aquinas, opusc. 57:1–4.

p. 126 Thomas à Kempis. From *The Imitation of Christ,* chaps. 1–2, bk. IV, trans. Ronald Knox and Michael Oakley (Burns and Oates, 1959).

p. 127 St. Francis de Sales. From *Athirst for God: Daily Readings with St. Francis de Sales,* ed. Michael Hollings (Darton, Longman and Todd, 1985).

p. 128 St. Rose Philippine Duchesne. From *Mother Philippine Duchesne,* by Marjory Erskine (Longmans, 1926), reproduced in *To Any Christian,* selected and arranged by a Benedictine of Stanbrook (Burns and Oates, 1964).

p. 128 Pierre Teilhard de Chardin. From *Hymn of the Universe,* by Pierre Teilhard de Chardin, English translation (New York: Harper and Row, 1965). © Georges Borchardt, Inc.

p. 130 Pope Paul VI. From a sermon preached in Manila, Philippines, on 29 November, 1970.

Pathways in Prayer

p. 132 St. Ephraem the Syrian. From the commentary of St. Ephraem the Syrian on the Diatessaron (the four Gospels in a single narrative), 1:18–19.

p. 133 Traditional Celtic blessing. "The Soul's Cry" is from *The Celtic Vision,* selections from the *Carmina Gadelica,* ed. Esther de Waal (Darton, Longman and Todd, 1988).

p. 134 St. Bernard of Clairvaux. A reading from the sermons of St. Bernard, De diversis 5:4–5.

p. 135 From *The Cloud of Unknowing.* From *The Cloud of Unknowing,* chap. 6, ed. James Walsh, S.J., Classics of Western Spirituality (New York: Paulist Press, 1981).

p. 135 Richard Rolle. From *Richard Rolle: The English Writings,* trans. and ed. by Rosamund S. Allen, Classics of Western Spirituality (New York: Paulist Press, 1988).

p. 136 Margery Kempe. From *The Mirror of Love: Daily Readings with Margery Kempe,* ed. Gillian Hawker (Darton, Longman and Todd, 1988).

p. 136 St. Francis de Sales. From *Athirst for God: Daily Readings with St. Francis de Sales,* ed. Michael Hollings (Darton, Longman and Todd, 1985).

p. 137 St. Rose of Lima. From the writings of St. Rose of Lima.

p. 138 St. Margaret Mary Alacoque. From the letters of St. Margaret Mary Alacoque.

p. 139 Jean-Pierre de Caussade. From *The Flame of Divine Love: Daily Readings with Jean-Pierre de Caussade,* ed. Robert Llewelyn (Darton, Longman and Todd, 1984).

p. 140 St. Jean-Baptiste Vianney. From the catechetical instructions of St. Jean-Baptiste Vianney.

p. 141 St. Thérèse of Lisieux. From *By Love Alone: Daily Readings with St. Thérèse of Lisieux,* ed. Michael Hollings (Darton, Longman and Todd, 1986).

p. 142 Marthe Robin. From *Marthe Robin,* by Raymond Peyret, trans. Clare Will Faulhaber (New York: Alba House, 1983).

p. 142 John Main. From *Moment of Christ,* by John Main (Darton, Longman and Todd, 1984).

Mystical Prayer

p. 145 St. Anselm of Canterbury. From *The Proslogion,* chap. 1, by St. Anselm. © The Clarendon Press, Oxford, for extracts from St. Anselm's *Proslogion,* trans. M. J. Charlesworth © Oxford University Press, 1965.

p. 147 St. Bernard of Clairvaux. From the sermons of St. Bernard of Clairvaux on the Song of Songs.

p. 147 Thomas à Kempis. From The *Imitation of Christ,* bk. 2, 1.1.

p. 171 St. Teresa of Ávila. From *Book of the Life,* by St. Teresa of Jesus, trans. E. Allison Peers, chap. 29, par. 13.

p. 150 St. John of the Cross. From *Dark Night,* in *Centred on Love: The Poems of St. John of the Cross,* trans. Marjorie Flower, O.C.D. (© 1983 The Carmelite Community, St. Andrew's Road, Varroville, NSW 2565, Australia), reproduced in *The Impact of God,* by Iain Matthew, O.C.D. (Hodder, 1995).

p. 151 Father Cholenec. From the contemporary biography of Kateri Tekakwitha, by Father Cholenec.

p. 152 Marie-Adele Garnier. From an unpublished account by Marie-Adele Garnier dated 1888. © Trustees Tyburn Benedictine Congregation.

p. 154 Thomas Dehau. Translated from the French in the journal *Jesus Caritas,* 1971.

p. 155 St. Thérèse of Lisieux. From Autobiography Ms C. 7v, taken from *By Love Alone: Daily Readings with Thérèse of Lisieux,* ed. Michael Hollings (Darton, Longman and Todd, 1986).

p. 156 Anthony de Mello. From *Sadhana: A Way to God,* by Anthony de Mello (St. Louis: Institute of Jesuit Sources, 1979).

Conversion and Call

p. 161 St. Athanasius. From the *Life of Antony,* chaps. 2–4, by St. Athanasius.

p. 162 Ronald Knox. From *Occasional Sermons of Ronald A. Knox,* preached in the Church of St. Anselm and St. Cecilia, Kingsway, London (Burns and Oates, 1960), slightly edited.

p. 163 "Test the Spirits." From the Acts of St. Ignatius, chap. I, 5–9, taken down by Luis Gonzalez.

p. 164 Mary Ward. A prayer of Mary Ward, reproduced in *Till God Will: Mary Ward through Her Writings,* ed. M. Emmanuel Orchard, I.B.V.M. (Darton, Longman and Todd, 1985).

p. 165 Venerable John Henry Newman.

p. 167 Francis Thompson.

p. 167 St. Thérèse of Lisieux. From the *Autobiography of St. Thérèse of Lisieux,* Ms B, 3r–3v, taken from *The Autobiography of a Saint,* trans. Ronald Knox, 1958. © The Executors of Ronald Knox.

p. 168 Dorothy Day. From *From Union Square to Rome,* by Dorothy Day (Silver Spring, Md.: Preservation of the Faith Press, 1938).

p. 169 Thomas Merton. From *Cistercian Life,* by Thomas Merton, p. 19.

States of Life

p. 171 St. John of Damascus.

p. 171 St. Bruno Hartenfaust. Statute 3.2 from *The Wound of Love* (Darton, Longman and Todd, 1994).

p. 172 Joseph Clayton. From *Hugh of Lincoln,* by Joseph Clayton (Burns, Oates and Washbourne, 1931).

p. 173 Conrad of Marburg. From a letter of Conrad of Marburg, St. Elizabeth of Hungary's spiritual director.

p. 174 Dante Alighieri. From *Inferno*, trans. Dorothy L. Sayers (David Higham Associates, 1947).

p. 175 St. Teresa of Ávila. From *The Way of Perfection*, by Teresa of Jesus, par. 2, 5, 6, taken from *Living Water: Daily Readings with St. Teresa of Ávila*, ed. Sister Mary, O.D.C. (Darton, Longman and Todd, 1986).

p. 176 "Lawrence of the Resurrection." From *An Oratory of the Heart: Daily Readings with Brother Lawrence of the Resurrection*, arranged and introduced by Robert Llewelyn (Darton, Longman and Todd, 1984).

p. 177 A seventeenth-century nun.

p. 178 Charles F. Mann. From *Madeleine Delbrêl: A Life beyond Boundaries*, by Charles F. Mann, taken from a review by Bill Griffin in the *Catholic Worker* newspaper.

p. 178 Joseph Bernardin. From Cardinal Joseph Bernardin's homily for his installation as archbishop of Chicago, 24 August 1982.

p. 178 Joseph Bernardin. From Cardinal Joseph Bernardin's final sermon to archdiocesan priests and religious on 7 October 1996 at Holy Name Cathedral, five weeks before his death on 13 November 1996. Reproduced in *The Gift of Peace: Personal Reflections by Joseph Cardinal Bernardin* (Loyola Press, 1997).

Marriage

p. 180 "Nuptial Blessing."

p. 181 Tertullian. From *Treatises on Marriage and Remarriage*, trans. William Le Saint, S.J., Ancient Christian Writers (Westminster, Md.: Newman Press, 1951).

p. 182 St. Augustine of Hippo. From *On Marriage and Concupiscence* 1.10 (PL 44. 420), taken from *A Patristic Breviary*, by Thomas Spidlik, trans. Paul Drake (London: New City Press, 1992).

p. 182 St. Francis de Sales. From *Athirst for God: Daily Readings with St. Francis de Sales*, ed. Michael Hollings (Darton, Longman and Todd, 1985).

p. 183 G. K. Chesterton. From "Boy and Girl: The Problem of Their Upbringing," *Daily Graphic*, 12 September 1907.

p. 184 Catherine de Hueck Doherty. From *Dear Parents,* by Catherine de Hueck Doherty (Madonna House Publications, Combermere, Ontario, Canada, 1997).

p. 186 William Johnston. From *Letters to Contemplatives* (Collins Fount, 1991).

p. 187 Margaret Grimer. From *Water into Wine* (Darton, Longman and Todd, 1986).

p. 187 Barbara Wood. © 1987 Barbara Wood.

Holy Living

p. 189 St. Augustine of Hippo. From the sermons of St. Augustine, sermon 256.

p. 190 Attributed to St. Francis of Assisi.

p. 191 "St. Francis of Assisi's True Joy." From *Francis of Assisi: Early Documents,* vol. I, *The Saint,* ed. Regis J. Armstrong, O.F.M. Cap., J. A. Wayne Hellmann, O.F.M. Conv., William J. Short, O.F.M. (London, New York, and the Philippines: New City Press). © 1999 Franciscan Institute of St. Bonaventure, New York.

p. 192 Thomas à Kempis. From *The Imitation of Christ.*

p. 193 Venerable John Henry Newman.

p. 193 Trelawney Saunders. From *Caroline Chisholm,* by Trelawney Saunders, taken from *The Emigrant's Friend,* by Joanna Bogle (Gracewing).

p. 194 Dorothy Day. From *On Pilgrimage: The Sixties.*

p. 195 F. A. Forbes. From *Margaret Sinclair,* by F. A. Forbes (London: Sands, 1927), slightly edited.

p. 195 Carlo Carretto. From *Love Is for Living* (Darton, Longman and Todd, 1976), taken from *God of the Impossible: Daily Readings with Carlo Carretto* (Darton, Longman and Todd, 1988).

p. 196 Mother Teresa of Calcutta. From *Something Beautiful for God,* by Malcolm Muggeridge (New York: Harper and Row, 1971).

Ministry

p. 200 St. Catherine of Siena. From *The Prayers of Catherine of Siena,* prayer 19, Passion Sunday, 27 March 1379, ed. Suzanne Noffke (New York: Paulist Press, 1983).

p. 201 St. Angela Merici. From *The Spiritual Testament of St. Angela Merici.*

p. 202 St. Francis Xavier. From the *Letters of St. Francis Xavier to St. Ignatius,* bk. 4, letter 4 (October 1542).

p. 203 St. Francis Xavier. From the *Letters of St. Francis Xavier to St. Ignatius,* bk. 4, letter 5 (January 1544).

p. 205 St. Peter Claver. From the *Letters of St. Peter Claver from Colombia,* letter to his auperior, 31 May 1627. Originally in Spanish in *San Pedro Claver,* ed. A. Valtierra, S.J. (Cartagena, 1964.)

p. 206 "Children Evangelize Children." Based on a letter from Nano Nagle to Miss FitzSimons in early 1770.

p. 206 Pope John XXIII. A reading from *Sacerdoti Nostri Primordia,* an encyclical of Pope John XXIII.

p. 208 St. John Bosco. From the letters of St. John Bosco, letter 4.

p. 209 St. Frances Xavier Cabrini. From a letter to "mia figlia carissima," 23 May 1904, reproduced in *Mother Cabrini,* by Mary Louise Sullivan, M.S.C. (Center for Migration Studies, 209 Flagg Pl., Staten Island, N.Y. 10304-1199, 1992).

p. 210 Frank Duff. From *Legio Mariae,* official handbook of the Legion of Mary, Dublin, 1993 (Concilium Legionis Mariae, de Montfort House, Morning Star Ave., Brunswick St., Dublin 7).

p. 210 Dorothy Day. From *On Pilgrimage: The Sixties.* Dated February 1968.

p. 211 Shusaku Endo. From *Silence,* by Shusaku Endo, trans. William Johnston (London: Peter Owen, 1976).

Spiritual Guidance

p. 213 St. Ambrose of Milan. From *Ambrose of Milan,* in Ps 1.33: CSEL 64, 28–30, taken from *Tradition Day by Day,* comp. and ed. John E. Rotelle (Augustinian Press, Villanova, Pa. 19085, 1994).

p. 214 St. Benedict of Nursia. From *The Rule of St. Benedict,* chaps. 3, 64, trans. and ed. Abbot Justin McCann (London: Sheed and Ward, 1951).

p. 215 St. Louis IX. From the spiritual testament of St. Louis to his son.

p. 216 Meister Eckhart. First paragraph from DW 83, DP 42 (W. 96. II.333). Second paragraph from DW 56, DP 6 (W. 13b, 1.117–18). Both reproduced in *Mysticism and Prophecy: The Dominican Tradition,* by Richard Woods, O.P. (Darton, Longman and Todd, 1998).

p. 216 St. John of the Cross. From *Living Flame,* 3.46., trans. Iain Matthew, O.C.D., in *The Impact of God,* by Iain Matthew, O.C.D. (Hodder, 1995).

p. 217 St. John of the Cross. From *The Dark Night of the Soul,* chap. 9, taken from *Lamps of Fire: Daily Readings with St. John of the Cross,* ed. Elizabeth Ruth Obbard, O.C.D. (Darton, Longman and Todd, 1985).

p. 217 Jean-Pierre de Caussade. From *The Sacrament of the Present Moment,* trans. Kitty Muggeridge (HarperCollins, 1981).

p. 218 Richard Challoner. From *Garden of the Soul* (1740).

p. 219 John Chapman. From *Spiritual Letters,* 2nd ed. (London: Sheed and Ward, 1935).

p. 220 Blessed Padre Pio. From letter of Passion Sunday, 29 March 1914, to Raffaelina Cerase, taken from *Correspondence,* vol. II (Editions "Padre Pio da Pietrelcina," 71013 San Giovanni Rotondo, Italy, 1997).

p. 220 Caryll Houselander. From *This War Is the Passion,* by Caryll Houselander (New York: Sheed and Ward, 1941).

p. 221 Thomas Philippe. From *The Contemplative Life,* ed. Edward D. O'Connor, C.S.C. (London: HarperCollins, 1991).

p. 222 Thomas Merton. From *No Man Is an Island* (Burns and Oates, 1955), taken from *The Shining Wilderness: Daily Readings with Thomas Merton* (Darton, Longman and Todd, 1988).

Spiritual Friendship

p. 224 St. Gregory of Nazianzus. From *Discourses of St. Gregory of Nazianzus,* or. 43.

p. 226 St. Gregory the Great. From a reading from *Dialogues of St. Gregory the Great,* bk. 2:33, 34.

p. 227 St. Anselm of Canterbury. From *Patrologia Latina* 158, ep. IV, col. 1098, reproduced in *To Any Christian,* selected and arranged by a Benedictine of Stanbrook (Burns and Oates, 1964).

p. 228 St. Aelred of Rievaulx. From *St. Aelred of Rievaulx: Spiritual Friendship* (Kalmazoo, Mich.: Cistercian Publications, 1977).

p. 229 Blessed Jordan of Saxony. From *To Heaven with Diana,* by Gerald Vann, a translation of the letters from Jordan of Saxony to the Dominican prioress Blessed Diana d'Andalo. © The Dominican Order in England.

p. 229 St. Thomas More. From a letter of St. Thomas More to his daughter Margaret Roper, written in 1534.

p. 230 St. Francis de Sales. Letter of 24 June 1604. From *Francis de Sales, Jane de Chantal: Letters of Spiritual Direction,* trans. Péronne Marie Thibert, Classics of Western Spirituality (New York: Paulist Press, 1988).

p. 231 Hilaire Belloc. From a letter to Katharine Asquith from Hilaire Belloc.

p. 232 St. Thérèse of Lisieux. From *Maurice and Thérèse,* trans. Patrick Ahern (Darton, Longman and Todd, 1999).

p. 233 Pope John Paul I. From *Illustrissimi: The Letters of Pope John Paul I* (London: Collins, 1978), slightly edited.

In Weakness, Strength

p. 238 St. John Chrysostom. On the letter to the Romans 21:1ff., (PG 60), taken from *A Patristic Breviary,* by Thomas Spidlik, trans. Paul Drake (London: New City Press, 1992).

p. 239 "St. Frances of Rome." From *The Life of St. Frances of Rome,* Acta Sanct. Martii 2, 188–89.

p. 239 Blessed Antoine Frédéric Ozanam. From a letter to Father Pendola, 19 July 1853. Reproduced in *Through the Eye of a Needle,* by Frédéric Ozanam (St. Pauls, 1989).

p. 240 Blessed Antoine Frédéric Ozanam. From the newspaper article "Alms-giving," *Ere Nouvelle,* 24 December 1848. Reproduced in *Through the Eye of a Needle,* by Frédéric Ozanam (St. Pauls, 1989).

p. 241 "Blessed Mary MacKillop." From the leaflet *The Australian People's Saint* (edited), used with permission of the Trustees of Sisters of St. Joseph of the Sacred Heart.

p. 242 Pope John XXIII. From *Journal of a Soul: John XXIII* (Geoffrey Chapman, a division of Cassell Ltd, 1980. Used by permission of Doubleday, a division of Random House, Inc.).

p. 242 Pope John XXIII. Headed "Thoughts in Solitude."

p. 243 Georges P. Vanier. From a letter to a Carmelite nun in 1959, taken from *In Weakness, Strength: The Spiritual Sources of Georges P. Vanier, 19th Governor-General of Canada,* by Jean Vanier (Toronto: Griffin House, 1969).

p. 244 Fulton Sheen.

p. 245 Pedro Arrupe. From *One Jesuit's Spiritual Journey: Autobiographical Conversations with Jean-Claude Dietsch* (St. Louis: Institute of Jesuit Sources, 1986).

p. 246 Donald Nicholl. From "Growing Old" (Priests and People, 1973).

p. 246 Henri J. M. Nouwen. From *The Inner Voice of Love* (Darton, Longman and Todd, 1996).

p. 247 "Love Me as You Are."

Martyrdom

p. 251 "United in Death." From the account of the martyrdom of the Holy Martyrs of Carthage, chaps. 18–21.

p. 251 "St. John Houghton and Companions."

p. 252 St. Edmund Campion. "Campion's Brag," 1580, addressed "To the Right Honourable the Lord's of her Majestie's Privy Council."

p. 253 "St. Paul Miki and Companions." From the account of the martyrdom of St. Paul Miki and his companions by a contemporary author. Acta Sanct.

p. 255 From the memoir of a secretary for St. Jane Frances de Chantal. From the memoir, III, ed. 1853.

p. 256 Pope John Paul II. From the homily of Pope John Paul II at the canonization of the Korean martyrs, 6 May 1984, reproduced in *Osservatore Romano*, English ed., 14 May 1984 (Via del Pellegrino 00120, Vatican City).

p. 256 Pope Paul VI. From an Angelus message of Pope Paul VI, reproduced in *Osservatore Romano*, 7 August 1969.

p. 257 Oscar Romero. From *Homilias*, vol. 4, 11 May 1978.

p. 258 Christian de Chergé. "Association des Ecrits des Septs de l'Atlas" (c/o Dom Andre Barbeau, O.C.S.O., Abbot Notre Dame d' Aiguebelle, Montjoyer, 26230, France).

Death and Eternity

p. 261 St. Ignatius of Antioch. From the letter of St. Ignatius of Antioch to the Romans, rom. 4, 1–2; 6, 1–8, 3.

p. 262 St. Augustine of Hippo. From *The Confessions of St. Augustine*, bk. IX. 10.23, trans. Maria Boulding (Hodder, 1997).

p. 262 St. Augustine of Hippo. From *The City of God*, by St. Augustine.

p. 263 Attributed to St. Bede the Venerable. "O God that art the only hope of the world" is sometimes attributed to Bede. From *The Oxford Book of Prayer*, ed. George Appleton (1985).

p. 263 St. Bede the Venerable. "I pray Thee, merciful Jesus" is from the end of Bede's *Historia Ecclesiastica*.

p. 264 St. Aloysius Gonzaga. From a letter of St. Aloysius Gonzaga to his mother, 10 June 1591, in "The Vocation of St. Aloysius Gonzaga," from *To Any Christian*, selected and arranged by a Benedictine of Stanbrook (Burns and Oates, 1964).

p. 265 Bede Griffiths. From "Prayer," a talk at Kreuth, Germany, 7 April 1992, reproduced in *Beyond the Darkness: A Biography of Bede Griffiths*, by Shirley du Boulay (Rider, 1998).

p. 266 Basil Hume. From *The Mystery of the Incarnation*, by Basil Hume (Darton, Longman and Todd, 1999).

p. 267 Flannery O'Connor. From "Revelation," in *Everything That Rises Must Converge* (New York: Farrar, Straus and Giroux, 1956).

pp. 4, 5, 10, 13, 20, 21, 22, 30, 31, 32, 36, 58, 67, 68, 69, 73, 87, 88, 93, 102, 108, 110, 111, 114, 121, 123, 124, 125, 132, 134, 137, 138, 140, 147, 161, 163, 171, 173, 189, 201, 205, 208, 215, 224, 226, 239, 251, 253, 255, 261 taken from the Divine Office. © A. P. Watt, Ltd, on behalf of the Hierarchies of England, Wales, Ireland and Australia, and Canada.

Every endeavor has been made to trace the copyright owners of each extract. There do, however, remain a few extracts for which the source is unknown to the compiler and the publisher. The publisher would be glad to hear from the copyright owners of the extracts, and due acknowledgment will be made in all future editions of the book.

AUTHORS AND SUBJECTS

Here is more information about the authors and texts quoted in this volume.

ST. ADAMNAN OF IONA (C. 625–704). Ninth abbot of Iona. Biographer of St. Columba. Feast day: September 23.

ST. AELRED OF RIEVAULX (C. 1110–67). Son of a Saxon priest. Cistercian abbot from 1147. Feast day: March 3.

ST. MARGARET MARY ALACOQUE (1647–90). French Visitandine nun and promoter of devotion to the Sacred Heart. Feast day: October 16.

ST. AMBROSE OF MILAN (C. 339–97). Bishop of Milan and instrumental in the conversion of St. Augustine. Doctor of the church. Feast day: December 7.

ST. ANDREW OF CRETE (C. 660–740). Theologian. Reputed to have invented the canon as a musical form. Feast day: July 4 (Eastern Church).

ST. ANSELM OF CANTERBURY (C. 1033–1109). Benedictine monk and reluctant archbishop of Canterbury from 1093. Doctor of the church. Feast day: April 21.

ST. ANTHONY OF EGYPT (C. 251–356). Hermit, "desert father," and the founder of monasticism. Feast day: January 17.

ST. THOMAS AQUINAS (C. 1225–74). Italian Dominican philosopher and theologian. Doctor of the church. Feast day: January 28.

PEDRO ARRUPE (1907–91). Basque superior general of the Jesuits (1965–81). Ministered to atomic-bomb victims at Hiroshima in 1945.

ST. ATHANASIUS (D. 373) Bishop of Alexandria from 328. Principal defender of Catholic orthodoxy against the Arians. Doctor of the church. Feast day: May 2.

ST. AUGUSTINE OF HIPPO (354–430). Bishop of Hippo in North Africa. Theologian and monastic founder. Doctor of the church. Feast day: August 28.

BALDWIN OF CANTERBURY (D. 1190). Monk of Forde. Archbishop of Canterbury from 1184.

ST. BASIL THE GREAT (C. 330–79). Cappadocian Father. Bishop of Caesarea from 370. Doctor of the church. Feast day: January 2 (with St. Gregory of Nazianzus).

ST. BEDE THE VENERABLE (C. 673–735). "The Father of English History." Benedictine monk of Jarrow. Doctor of the church. Feast day: May 25.

HILAIRE BELLOC (1870–1953). French-born English poet and writer.

ST. BENEDICT OF NURSIA (C. 480–C. 547). "Patriarch of Western Monasticism." Italian founder of the Benedictines. Feast day: July 11.

ST. BERNADETTE OF LOURDES (1844–79). French peasant girl to whom the Blessed Virgin appeared. Feast day: April 16.

ST. BERNARD OF CLAIRVAUX (1090–1153). French Cistercian abbot who exercised immense influence. Doctor of the church. Feast day: August 20.

JOSEPH BERNARDIN (1928–96). Cardinal archbishop of Chicago. Recipient of the Medal of Freedom in 1996.

BIANCO DA SIENA (D. 1412). Italian mystical poet.

ST. BONAVENTURE (C. 1217–74). Italian Franciscan theologian. Minister general of the order from 1257. Doctor of the church. Feast day: July 15.

ST. BONIFACE (C. 675–754). "Apostle of Germany." Born in England. Martyred in 754. Feast day: June 5.

ST. JOHN BOSCO (1815–88). Founded the Salesian order near Turin for the care of boys. Feast day: January 31.

JOHN BRADBURNE (1921–79). English Franciscan tertiary. Died in Zimbabwe defending those suffering from leprosy.

RAYMOND E. BROWN (1928–98). Sulpician priest born in New York. Outstanding New Testament scholar.

ST. BRUNO HARTENFAUST (C. 1030–1101). Born in Germany. With six companions, founded the Carthusian order near Grenoble in 1084. Feast day: October 6.

ST. FRANCES XAVIER CABRINI (1850–1917). Italian missionary to American immigrants. First U.S. citizen to be canonized. Feast day: November 13.

ST. CAESARIUS OF ARLES (C. 470–542). Monk of the island of Lerins. Archbishop of Arles at the age of thirty-three. Feast day: August 27.

ST. EDMUND CAMPION (1540–81). One of the first Jesuits to return to England. Martyred at Tyburn. Feast day: December 1.

CARLO CARRETTO (1910–88). Italian youth leader who subsequently became a priest and a follower of Charles de Foucauld.

ST. CATHERINE OF SIENA (C. 1347–80). Influential Italian Dominican tertiary and mystic. Doctor of the church. Feast day: April 29.

JEAN-PIERRE DE CAUSSADE (1675–1751). French Jesuit known for his book *Self-Abandonment to Divine Providence*.

CELTIC TRADITION (C. 500–C. 800). Of the churches without insititutional unity in the areas where Celtic languages were spoken.

RICHARD CHALLONER (1691–1781). Vicar apostolic from 1758 and thus responsible for the Catholic community in England.

ST. JANE FRANCES DE CHANTAL (1572–1641). As a widow, cofounded the Visitation Order in France. Feast day: December 12.

JOHN CHAPMAN (1865–1933). English Benedictine monk and author. Abbot of Downside from 1929.

CHRISTIAN DE CHERGÉ (1937–96). French Cistercian prior martyred in Algeria with six others.

G. K. CHESTERTON (1874–1936). English author, journalist, and champion of Catholic orthodoxy.

CAROLINE CHISHOLM (1808–77). Devoted her life to the care of women emigrating to Australia from England.

ST. JOHN CHRYSOSTOM (C. 349–407). Patriarch of Constantinople whose last name means "golden mouth." Doctor of the church. Feast day: September 13.

PAUL CLAUDEL (1868–1955). Playwright and diplomat. French ambassador to Washington (1926–33).

ST. PETER CLAVER (1581–1654). Spanish Jesuit missionary to black slaves in Colombia. Feast day: September 9.

THE CLOUD OF UNKNOWING **(FOURTEENTH CENTURY).** Anonymous contemplative work.

ST. COLUMBA (521–97). In Irish, *Colum Cille,* or "dove of the church." Columba founded the monastery on Iona. Feast day: June 9.

ST. COLUMBANUS (C. 543–615). Irish missionary. Worked in France, Germany, and Italy. Feast day: November 23.

CONRAD OF MARBURG (C. 1180–1233). Spiritual director of St. Elizabeth of Hungary.

CYNEWULF (NINTH CENTURY). Anglo-Saxon religious poet.

ST. CYRIL OF ALEXANDRIA (C. 375–444). Patriarch of Alexandria and theologian. Opposed the teaching of Nestorius. Doctor of the church. Feast day: June 27.

DANTE ALIGHIERI (1265–1321). Italian poet and philosopher. Author of *The Divine Comedy.*

DOROTHY DAY (1897–1980). Prominent American pacifist, journalist, and social activist.

ANTHONY DE MELLO (1931–87). Indian Jesuit author, retreat giver, and spiritual director.

THOMAS DEHAU (1870–1956). French Dominican theologian and spiritual director.

MADELEINE DELBRÊL (1904–64). With her companions lived alongside the poor in the Paris suburb of Ivry.

DIADOCHUS OF PHOTICE (FIFTH CENTURY). Bishop of Photice after 451.

LETTER TO DIOGNETUS (C. SECOND CENTURY). Letter from an unknown Christian to an otherwise unknown inquirer.

CATHERINE DE HUECK DOHERTY (1900–1985). Russian-born American founder of the Madonna House lay apostolate in Canada.

ST. DOMINIC DE GUZMAN (C. 1170–1221). Spanish founder of the Order of Friars Preacher (1215). Feast day: August 8.

"THE DREAM OF THE ROOD." Old English poem by an unknown author representing the feelings of the cross during the Crucifixion.

ST. ROSE PHILIPPINE DUCHESNE (1769–1852). First member of the Society of the Sacred Heart to go on a mission from France to America in 1818. Feast day: November 18.

FRANK DUFF (1889–1980). Dublin-born founder of the Legion of Mary (1921).

MEISTER ECKHART (C. 1260–C. 1328). German Dominican theologian. Accused of heresy in 1326 and died denying the charges.

ST. ELIZABETH OF HUNGARY (1207–31). Daughter of the King of Hungary. Devoted herself to the sick. Feast day: November 17.

BLESSED ELIZABETH OF THE TRINITY (1880–1906). French Carmelite of Dijon. Feast day: November 8.

SHUSAKU ENDO (1923–96). Japanese novelist.

ST. EPHRAEM THE SYRIAN (C. 306–73). Bible scholar and hymn writer. Doctor of the church. Feast day: June 9.

EXULTET (SEVENTH/EIGHTH CENTURY). Paschal proclamation sung on Holy Saturday night.

ST. FELICITY (D. 203). African slave. Martyred at Carthage with St. Perpetua. Their feast day: March 7.

CHARLES DE FOUCAULD (1858–1916). French explorer known as "the Hermit of the Sahara." His rule has attracted many followers.

ST. FRANCES OF ROME (1384–1440). Widow. Founded a community of Benedictine oblates. Feast day: March 9.

ST. FRANCIS DE SALES (1567–1622). Bishop of Geneva from 1602. Cofounder of the Visitation Order. Doctor of the church. Feast day: January 24.

ST. FRANCIS OF ASSISI (C. 1181–1226). Founder of the Franciscans (1209). Deeply committed to the poor. Feast day: October 4.

MARIE-ADELE GARNIER (1838–1924). French founder of the Adorers of the Sacred Heart of Montmartre, a Benedictine congregation.

ST. GERTRUDE THE GREAT (C. 1256–C. 1302). German mystic and visionary. Nun of Helfta. Feast day: November 16.

ST. ALOYSIUS GONZAGA (1568–91). Italian Jesuit novice. Died of plague in Rome at age twenty-three. Feast day: June 21.

ST. GREGORY OF NAZIANZUS (C. 329–90). Cappadocian Father. Son of the bishop of Nazianzus. Doctor of the church. Feast day: January 2 (with St. Basil).

ST. GREGORY OF NYSSA (C. 335–C. 395). Cappadocian Father. Bishop of Nyssa. Brother of St. Basil. Feast day: March 9.

ST. GREGORY THE GREAT (C. 540–604). Pope from 590. Sent St. Augustine to England in 596. Doctor of the church. Feast day: September 3.

BEDE GRIFFITHS (1906–93). English Benedictine monk. In India, became known as a bridge between East and West.

MARGARET GRIMER (1933–95). Worked for many years with the Catholic Marriage Advisory Council in England.

ST. HILDEGARD OF BINGEN (1098–1179). German mystic and Benedictine abbess. Feast day: September 17.

GERARD MANLEY HOPKINS (1844–89). English Jesuit poet and professor of Greek in Dublin.

CARYLL HOUSELANDER (1901–54). English writer, poet, and artist.

FRIEDRICH VON HÜGEL (1852–1925). Baron, theologian, and philosopher.

ST. HUGH OF LINCOLN (C. 1140–1200). French Carthusian who became Bishop of Lincoln. Feast day: November 17.

BASIL HUME (1923–99). English Benedictine monk. Abbot of Ampleforth (1963–76). Cardinal archbishop of Westminster (1976–99).

ST. IGNATIUS OF ANTIOCH (C. 35–C. 107). Bishop of Antioch. Martyred in Rome. Feast day: October 17.

ST. IGNATIUS OF LOYOLA (1491–1556). Spanish soldier. Founder of the Society of Jesus (1540). Feast day: July 31.

ISAAC OF NINEVEH (D. C. 700). Monk and bishop of Nineveh.

ST. JOHN OF DAMASCUS (C. 675–C. 749). Theologian and hymn writer. Doctor of the church. Feast day: December 4.

ST. JOHN OF THE CROSS (1542–91). Spanish mystic and co-reformer of the Discalced Carmelites. Doctor of the church. Feast day: December 14.

JOHN PAUL I (1912–78). Pope from August 26 to September 28, 1978.

JOHN PAUL II (B. 1920). Pope from 1978.

JOHN XXIII (1881–1963). Pope from 1958. Convened the Second Vatican Council (1962–65).

WILLIAM JOHNSTON (B. 1925). Irish-born Jesuit living and working in Japan. Prominent in Buddhist-Christian dialogue.

BLESSED JORDAN OF SAXONY (C. 1190–1237). German master general of the Dominican order from 1222. Feast day: February 13.

JULIAN OF NORWICH (C. 1342–C. 1420). English anchoress and spiritual writer.

MARGERY KEMPE (C. 1373–AFTER 1433). English visionary, author, and mother of fourteen children.

RONALD KNOX (1888–1957). English priest, scholar, and translator of the Bible.

ST. MAXIMILIAN KOLBE (1894–1941). Polish Franciscan. Died in Auschwitz. Feast day: August 14.

KOREAN MARTYRS (1784–1839). The more than ten thousand martyrs of the laity-founded Korean Church. Feast day: September 21.

LAWRENCE OF THE RESURRECTION (1614–91). French Carmelite laybrother and mystic.

St. Leo the Great (d. 461). Leo I. Pope from 440. Doctor of the church. Feast day: November 10.

Bernard Lonergan (1904–84). Canadian Jesuit theologian, philosopher, and economist.

St. Louis IX (1214–70). King of France, crowned 1226. Feast day: August 25.

Blessed Mary MacKillop (1842–1909). Foundress of the first Australian religious order, The Sisters of Joseph. Feast day: August 8.

John Main (1926–82). Irish-born Benedictine monk and founder of the Christian Meditation movement.

Blessed Marie of the Incarnation (1599–1672). French missionary to the Huron in Canada. Feast day: April 30.

St. Martin de Porres (1579–1639). Peruvian Dominican lay brother who cared for the poor. Feast day: November 3.

St. Martin of Tours (c. 316–97). Bishop of Tours and a patron saint of France. Feast day: November 11.

St. Melito of Sardis (d. c. 190). Bishop of Sardis and prolific writer. Feast day: April 1.

St. Angela Merici (1474–1540). Italian founder of the Ursulines, the first congregation for the education of girls. Feast day: January 27.

Thomas Merton (1915–68). Influential American Cistercian monk and writer.

St. Paul Miki (d. 1597). Japanese Jesuit martyr. Feast day: February 6.

St. Louis Grignion de Montfort (1673–1716). French mission preacher and founder of the Montfort Fathers. Author of *True Devotion to Mary.* Feast day: April 28.

St. Thomas More (1478–1535). Martyr. Lord chancellor of England (1529–32). Feast day: June 22 (with St. John Fisher).

Nano Nagle (c. 1718–84). Prominent Irish educationalist and founder of the Sisters of the Presentation of the Blessed Virgin Mary.

VENERABLE JOHN HENRY NEWMAN (1801–90). Established the Oratorians in England (1849). Cardinal from 1879.

DONALD NICHOLL (1923–97). English scholar. First rector of the Ecumenical Institute at Tantur outside Bethlehem.

HENRI J. M. NOUWEN (1932–96). Dutch American priest, writer, teacher, and spiritual director.

FLANNERY O'CONNOR (1925–64). American writer born in Savannah, Georgia.

ST. JOHN OGILVIE (C. 1579–1615). Scots Jesuit. Martyred in Glasgow. Feast day: March 10.

BLESSED ANTOINE FRÉDÉRIC OZANAM (1813–53). French scholar and founder of the Society of St. Vincent de Paul. Feast day: September 9.

BLESSED PADRE PIO (1887–1968). Italian Franciscan priest and mystic. Feast day: September 23.

ST. PATRICK (C. 390–C. 461). "Apostle to the Irish." Feast day: March 17.

PAUL VI (1897–1978). Pope from 1963.

ST. MARY MAGDALEN DEI PAZZI (1566–1607). Italian Carmelite mystic. Feast day: May 25.

CHARLES PÉGUY (1873–1914). French poet and philosopher.

ST. PERPETUA (D. 203). African martyr. Died in Carthage with St. Felicity. Their feast day: March 7.

THOMAS PHILIPPE (1905–93). French Dominican theologian. Cofounder of the Communities of L'Arche (1964).

PSEUDO-DIONYSIUS THE AREOPAGITE (FIFTH/SIXTH CENTURY). So called because the writings of the otherwise unknown author were at one time ascribed to the first-century convert Dionysius the Areopagite (Acts 17:34).

KARL RAHNER (1904–84). Influential German Jesuit theologian. Prominent at the Second Vatican Council.

RICHARD OF ST. VICTOR (D. 1173). Scots theologian who lived and taught at the abbey of St. Victor in Paris.

MARTHE ROBIN (1902–81). Mystic who greatly influenced twentieth-century French religious communities.

RICHARD ROLLE (C. 1300–49). English hermit and spiritual writer.

OSCAR ROMERO (1917–80). Archbishop of San Salvador from 1977. Murdered while celebrating Mass in his diocese.

ST. ROSE OF LIMA (1586–1617). Peruvian of Spanish origin. Dominican tertiary. Feast day: August 23.

ST. SCHOLASTICA (C. 480–543). Benedictine nun. Sister of St. Benedict. Feast day: February 10.

BLESSED JOHN DUNS SCOTUS (C. 1266–1308). Scottish Franciscan philosopher and theologian. Feast day: November 8.

FULTON SHEEN (1895–1979). American archbishop. Popular writer, preacher, and radio and television speaker.

VENERABLE MARGARET SINCLAIR (1900–25). Edinburgh working girl who became a Poor Clare in England.

ST. ROBERT SOUTHWELL (1561–95). English Jesuit poet and martyr. Feast day: February 21.

ST. EDITH STEIN (1891–1942). Jewish-born philosopher and Carmelite nun. Died in Auschwitz. Feast day: August 9.

PIERRE TEILHARD DE CHARDIN (1881–1955). French Jesuit theologian and scientist.

BLESSED KATERI TEKAKWITHA (1656–80). Native American convert who practiced great personal austerity. Feast day: April 17.

ST. TERESA OF ÁVILA (1515–82). Spanish mystic and co-reformer of the Discalced Carmelites. Doctor of the church. Feast day: October 15.

MOTHER TERESA OF CALCUTTA (1910–97). Born of an Albanian family in Skopje (Macedonia). Founder of the Missionaries of Charity (1950).

TERTULLIAN (C. 160–C. 225). African church father.

ST. THÉRÈSE OF LISIEUX (1873–97). French Carmelite. A patron saint of France. Doctor of the church. Feast day: October 1.

THOMAS À KEMPIS (C. 1380–1471). Dutch Augustinian canon. Author of the *Imitation of Christ*.

FRANCIS THOMPSON (1859–1907). English mystical poet.

UGANDA MARTYRS (1885–86). Protestants and Catholics from the age of fifteen (St. Kizito) martyred by the ruler, Mwanga. Feast day: June 3.

GEORGES P. VANIER (1888–1967). Soldier and diplomat. Governor-general of Canada from 1959 to 1967.

BLESSED JOSEPH DE VEUSTER (FATHER DAMIEN OF MOLOKAI, 1840–89). Belgian missionary to leprosy sufferers on the Hawaiian island of Molokai. Beatified in 1995. Feast day: May 10.

ST. JEAN-BAPTISTE VIANNEY (1786–1859). From 1818, renowned parish priest of Ars in France. Feast day: August 4.

ST. VINCENT DE PAUL (1580–1660). French servant of the poor. Founded the Sisters of Charity and the Congregation of the Mission (Vincentians). Feast day: September 27.

TONY WALSH (1898–1994). Taught Native American children and founded Labre House for the homeless of Montreal.

MARY WARD (1585–1645). English educator and founder of the Institute of the Blessed Virgin Mary.

BARBARA WOOD (B. 1946). English writer whose work includes a biography of her father, the economist E. F. Schumacher.

ST. FRANCIS XAVIER (1506–52). Basque "Apostle of the Indies and of Japan." One of the first Jesuits. Feast day: December 3.

INDEX

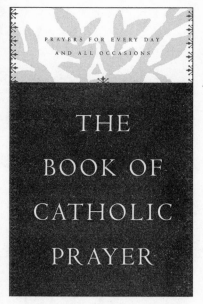